I ⟨GO⟩ WITH THEE
AND BE THY GUIDE,
IN THY MOST NEED
TO GO BY THY SIDE

EVERYMAN'S LIBRARY
POCKET POETS

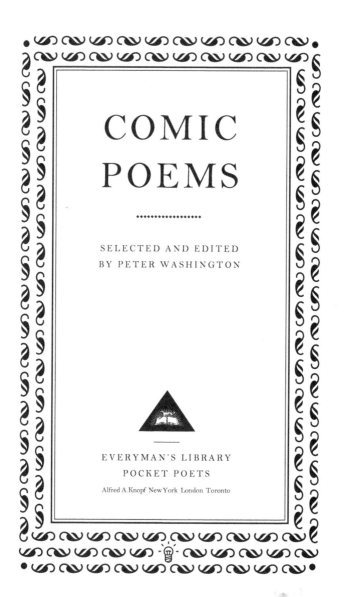

COMIC
POEMS

....

SELECTED AND EDITED
BY PETER WASHINGTON

EVERYMAN'S LIBRARY
POCKET POETS

Alfred A. Knopf New York London Toronto

THIS IS A BORZOI BOOK
PUBLISHED BY ALFRED A. KNOPF

This selection by Peter Washington first published in
Everyman's Library, 2001
Copyright © 2001 by Everyman's Library

Seventh printing (US)

All rights reserved. Published in the United States by Alfred A. Knopf,
a division of Penguin Random House LLC, New York, and in Canada by
Penguin Random House Canada Ltd., Toronto. Distributed by Penguin
Random House LLC, New York. Published in the United Kingdom by
Everyman's Library, 50 Albemarle Street, London W1S 4DB, and
distributed by Penguin Random House UK,
20 Vauxhall Bridge Road, London SW1V 2SA.

www.randomhouse.com/everymans
www.everymanslibrary.co.uk

ISBN 978-0-375-41354-4 (US)
978-1-84159-747-8 (UK)

A CIP catalogue record for this book is available from the British Library

Typography by Peter B. Willberg
Typeset in the UK by AccComputing, North Barrow, Somerset
Printed and bound in Germany by GGP Media GmbH, Pössneck

CONTENTS

LIMERICKS AND CLERIHEWS

7

NONSENSE AND WORD-PLAY

Part Two: Themes
LOVE AND MARRIAGE

SOME PAINS AND PLEASURES

LITERATURE

BESTIARY

Part One: Forms
SHORTS

NEWS ITEM

Men seldom make passes
At girls who wear glasses.

DOROTHY PARKER

Wig, rouge, honey, wax, teeth:
with a make-up bill like yours
you'd save money buying a face.

LUCILIUS
TRANS. PETER PORTER

THEIR SEX LIFE

One failure on
Top of another.

A. R. AMMONS

EPIGRAM VI.57

With fictive locks and scented glue
    You hide your dome: who's fooling who?
A haircut? That's a simple matter.
    No clippers, please; just soap and water.

MARTIAL, TRANS. DUDLEY FITTS

EPIGRAM IX.33

Outside the Baths you hear applause –
Flaccus, you know the likely cause.
Connoisseurs love fine workmanship,
Maron has let his towel slip.

MARTIAL, TRANS. PETER PORTER

BOSTON

I come from the city of Boston,
The home of the bean and the cod,
Where Cabots speak only to Lowells,
And Lowells speak only to God.

SAMUEL C. BUSHNELL

Diophon, seeing
another man
crucified on
a higher cross
than him, died
of envy.

Hermogenes is rather short,
He looks up microbes' mini-skirts,
And high above him, snowy-topped,
Loom peaks of objects that he's dropped.

LUCILIUS
TRANS. PETER PORTER

A CASE

As I was going up the stair
I met a man who wasn't there.
He wasn't there again today –
I wish to God he'd go away!

TWINS

Siamese twins: one, maddened by
The other's moral bigotry,
Resolved at length to misbehave
And drink them both into the grave.

ROBERT GRAVES

Busts and bosoms have I known
  Of various shapes and sizes
From grievous disappointments
  To jubilant surprises.

ANON.

I like a woman built on ample lines,
A Daimler of a girl or a Dowager –
One gives a well-sprung ride, the other
Makes *you* the plat-du-jour when she dines!

NIKARCHOS, TRANS. PETER PORTER

THIS ENGLISHWOMAN

This Englishwoman is so refined
She has no bosom and no behind.

FATIGUE

I'm tired of Love: I'm still more tired of Rhyme.
But Money gives me pleasure all the time.

HILAIRE BELLOC

VARIATION ON BELLOC'S 'FATIGUE'

I hardly ever tire of love or rhyme –
That's why I'm poor and have a rotten time.

WENDY COPE

RÉSUMÉ

Razors pain you;
Rivers are damp;
Acids stain you;
And drugs cause cramp.
Guns aren't lawful;
Nooses give;
Gas smells awful;
You might as well live.

DOROTHY PARKER

Mean old Hermon
dreamt he'd spent
all his money
and hanged himself
for fear of
dreaming it again.

LUCILIUS, TRANS. PETER PORTER

THE HARDSHIP OF ACCOUNTING

Never ask of money spent
Where the spender thinks it went.
Nobody was ever meant
To remember or invent
What he did with every cent.

ROBERT FROST

EPIGRAM

To John I ow'd great obligation;
   But John unhappily thought fit
To publish it to all the nation:
   So John and I are more than quit.

 MATTHEW PRIOR

HUMAN LIFE

What trifling coil do we poor mortals keep;
Wake, eat, and drink, evacuate, and sleep.

MATTHEW PRIOR

CHERRY WHITE

I never see that prettiest thing –
A cherry bough gone white with Spring –
But what I think, 'How gay 'twould be
To hang me from a flowering tree.'

SOME ARE BORN

Some are born to peace and joy
And some are born to sorrow
But only for a day as we
Shall not be here tomorrow.

STEVIE SMITH

COMMON SENSE

Why did the Lord give us agility
If not to evade responsibility?

OGDEN NASH

THE QUESTION

Yes, yes, I grant the sons of earth
Are doom'd to trouble from their birth.
We all of sorrow have our share;
But say, is yours without compare?

COMPANY

Where two or three
are gathered together, that
is about enough.

LES MURRAY

SAMSON AGONISTES

I test my bath before I sit,
And I'm always moved to wonderment
That what chills the finger not a bit
Is so frigid upon the fundament.

OGDEN NASH

Man stole fire, and Zeus created flame
much fiercer still; Woman was its name.

Fire's soon put out, but women blaze
like volcanic conflagrations all our days.

PALLADAS
TRANS. TONY HARRISON

Having slept with a man
the grammarian's daughter
gave birth to a child, in turn
masculine, feminine & neuter.

PALLADAS
TRANS. PETER JAY

PROPHETIC SOUL

Because your eyes are slant and slow,
   Because your hair is sweet to touch,
My heart is high again; but oh,
   I doubt if this will get me much.

DOROTHY PARKER

TWO CURES FOR LOVE

1   Don't see him. Don't phone or write a letter.
2   The easy way: get to know him better.

Eutychus the painter
Fathered twenty sons.
And did he get a likeness?
    Not once!

LUCILIUS
TRANS. ALISTAIR ELLIOT

REFLECTION ON ICE-BREAKING

Candy
Is dandy
But liquor
Is quicker.

GENEALOGICAL REFLECTION

No McTavish
Was ever lavish.

REMINISCENT REFLECTION

When I consider how my life is spent,
I hardly ever repent.

CROSSING THE BORDER

Senescence begins
And middle age ends
The day your descendants
Outnumber your friends.

EPIGRAM II.38

You wonder if my farm pays me its share?
It pays me this: I do not see you there.

MARTIAL, TRANS. RAYMOND OLIVER

ON RUTT THE JUDGE

Rutt, to the Suburb Beauties full well known,
Was from the bag scarce crept into a Gown,
When he, by telling of himself fine tales,
Was made a Judge, and sent away to *Wales*:
'Twas proper and most fit it should be so,
Whither should Goats but to the Mountains go?

CHARLES COTTON

TREASON

Treason doth never prosper – What's the reason?
If it doth prosper, none dare call it treason.

ON CERTAIN LADIES

When other fair ones to the shades go down,
Still Chloe, Flavia, Delia, stay in town:
Those ghosts of beauty wandering here reside,
And haunt the places where their honour died.

ALEXANDER POPE

ON TAKING A WIFE

'Come, come,' said Tom's father, 'at your time of life,
   There's no longer excuse for thus playing the rake.
It's time you should think, boy, of taking a wife.'
   'Why so it is, father. Whose wife shall I take?'

THOMAS MOORE

SWANS SING BEFORE THEY DIE

Swans sing before they die – 'twere no bad thing
Should certain persons die before they sing.

JULIET

How did the party go in Portman Square?
I cannot tell you; Juliet was not there.
And how did Lady Gaster's party go?
Juliet was next me and I do not know.

HILAIRE BELLOC

THE REWARD

In my mind's reception room
Which is what, and who is whom?
I notice when the candle's lighted
Half the guests are uninvited,
And oddest fancies, merriest jests,
Come from these unbidden guests.

LIMERICKS AND CLERIHEWS

RELATIVITY

There was a young lady named Bright,
Who travelled much faster than light,
    She started one day
    In the relative way,
And returned on the previous night.

MIND AND MATTER

There was a faith-healer of Deal,
Who said, 'Although pain isn't real,
    If I sit on a pin
    And it punctures my skin,
I dislike what I fancy I feel.'

DETERMINISM

There was a young man who said, 'Damn!
It appears to me now that I am
    Just a being that moves
    In predestinate grooves,
Not a taxi or bus, but a tram.'

ANON.

A young schizophrenic named Struther,
When told of the death of his brother,
   Said: 'Yes, it's too bad,
   But I can't feel too sad –
After all, I still have each other.'

ANON.

IDEALISM

There once was a man who said, 'God
Must think it exceedingly odd
   If he finds that this tree
   Continues to be
When there's no one about in the Quad.'

RONALD KNOX

A REPLY

Dear Sir, Your astonishment's odd,
I am always about in the Quad;
   And that's why this tree
   Will continue to be,
Since observed by Yours faithfully, GOD.

There was a young lady of Riga
Who went for a ride on a tiger:
    They returned from the ride
    With the lady inside
And a smile on the face of the tiger.

*

There was an old man of Boulogne
Who sang a most topical song.
    It wasn't the words
    Which frightened the birds,
But the horrible double entendre.

*

There was an old party of Lyme
Who married three wives at one time.
    When asked: 'Why the third?'
    He replied: 'One's absurd,
And bigamy, sir, is a crime.'

*

When Daddy and Mum got quite plastered,
And their shame had been thoroughly mastered,
    They told their boy, Harry:
    'Son, we never *did* marry.
But don't tell the neighbours, you bastard.'

ANON.

BUMP!

Things that go 'bump' in the night
Should not really give one a fright.
It's the hole in each ear
That lets in the fear,
That, and the absence of light!

SPIKE MILLIGAN

DRUSILLA

There was an old man of Schoharie
Who settled himself in a quarry.
And those who asked why
Got the candid reply,
'Today is the day of the soirée.'

ÉDOUARD

A bugler named Dougal MacDougal
Found ingenious ways to be frugal.
He learned how to sneeze
In various keys,
Thus saving the price of a bugle.

ARTHUR

There was an old man of Calcutta
Who coated his tonsils with butta,
Thus converting his snore
From a thunderous roar
To a soft, oleaginous mutta.

BENJAMIN

There was a brave girl of Connecticut
Who flagged the express with her pecticut,
Which her elders defined
As presence of mind,
But deplorable absence of ecticut.

CARLOTTA

There was an old man in a trunk
Who inquired of his wife, 'Am I drunk?'
She replied with regret,
'I'm afraid so, my pet,'
And he answered, 'It's just as I thunk.'

REQUIEM

There was a young belle of old Natchez
Whose garments were always in patchez.
When comment arose
On the state of her clothes,
She drawled, When Ah itchez, Ah scratchez!

OGDEN NASH

A Young Person came out of the mists,
Who had the most beautiful wrists:
    A scandal occurred
    Which has long been interred,
But the legend about them persists.

As the poets have mournfully sung,
Death takes the innocent young,
    The rolling in money,
    The screamingly funny,
And those who are very well hung.

LIMERICKS

There was an Old Man with a beard,
Who said, 'It is just as I feared! –
    Two Owls and a Hen,
    Four Larks and a Wren,
Have all built their nests in my beard!'

There was an Old Lady of Chertsey,
Who made a remarkable curtsey;
She twirled round and round, till she sunk
     underground,
Which distressed all the people of Chertsey.

There was an Old Man whose despair
Induced him to purchase a hare:
Whereon one fine day, he rode wholly away,
Which partly assuaged his despair.

There was an Old Man who said, 'Hush!
I perceive a young bird in this bush!'
    When they said , 'Is it small?'
    He replied, 'Not at all!
It is four times as big as the bush!'

EDWARD LEAR

NOMENCLATURIK

There was a young fellow named Cholmondeley,
Whose bride was so mellow and colmondeley
That the best man, Colquhoun,
An inane young bolqufoun,
Could only stand still and stare dolmondeley.

The bridgeroom's first cousin, young Belvoir,
Whose dad was a Lancashire welvoir,
Arrived with George Bohun
At just about nohun
When excitement was mounting to felvoir.

The vicar – his surname was Beauchamp –
Of marriage endeavoured to teauchamp,
While the bridesmaid, Miss Marjoribanks,
Played one or two harjoripranks;
But the shoe that she threw failed to reauchamp.

OSCAR WILDE

If, with the literate, I am
Impelled to try an epigram,
I never seek to take the credit;
We all assume that Oscar said it.

D. G. ROSSETTI

Dante Gabriel Rossetti
Buried all of his *libretti*,
Thought the matter over – then
Went and dug them up again.

ALEXANDRE DUMAS
AND HIS SON

Although I work, and seldom cease,
At Dumas *père* and Dumas *fils*,
Alas, I cannot make me care
For Dumas *fils* and Dumas *père*.

GEORGE GISSING

When I admit neglect of Gissing,
They say I don't know what I'm missing.
Until their arguments are subtler,
I think I'll stick to Samuel Butler.

WALTER SAVAGE LANDOR

Upon the work of Walter Landor
I am unfit to write with candor.
If you can read it, well and good;
But as for me, I never could.

From BIOGRAPHY FOR BEGINNERS

John Stuart Mill,
By a mighty effort of will,
Overcame his natural bonhomie
And wrote 'Principles of Political Economy'.

The intrepid Ricardo,
With characteristic bravado,
Alluded openly to Rent
Wherever he went.

'No, sir,' said General Sherman,
'I did *not* enjoy the sermon;
Nor I didn't git any
Kick outer the Litany.'

George the Third
Ought never to have occurred.
One can only wonder
At so grotesque a blunder.

Adam Smith
Was disowned by all his kith,
But he was backed through thick and thin
By all his kin.

From ACADEMIC GRAFFITI
In Memoriam Ogden Nash

Lord Byron
Once succumbed to a Siren:
His flesh was weak,
Hers Greek.

Henry Adams
Was mortally afraid of Madams:
In a disorderly house
He sat quiet as a mouse.

Henry James
Abhorred the word *Dames,*
And always wrote, *'Mommas'*
With inverted commas.

When Karl Marx
Found the phrase 'financial sharks',
He sang a Te Deum
In the British Museum.

Cardinal Newman
Was being only human
When he dreamed of panning
The latest contract by Cardinal Manning.

NONSENSE AND
WORD-PLAY

B   KW RM

Hated by the Muses!
serial eater!
mutilat r!
living in a h le,
feeding n st len qu tati ns –
why d y u lie in ambush (blackskin)
graving y ur spiteful image
in my h ly *Numbers*?
B kw rm!
fly fr m the Muses –
far away –
keeping y ur evil l   ks
  ff the g   d acc unt
  f my arithmetic b   ks!

EUENOS
TRANS. ALISTAIR ELLIOT

LAPSUS LINGUAE

We wanted Li Wing
    But we winged Willie Wong.
A sad but excusable
    Slip of the tong.

KEITH PRESTON   51

FAULTS

Shun these six faults to win success:
    Sleep, sloth,
    Fear, wrath.
Sl ove nlin es s'   l o n g w i n d e d n e s s.

AMARU
TRANS. JOHN BROUGH

       40-   LOVE

    MIDDLE   aged
    couple   playing
    ten   nis
    when   the
    game   ends
    and   they
    go   home
    the   net
    will   still
    be   be
    tween   them

TENUOUS AND PRECARIOUS

Tenuous and Precarious
Were my guardians,
Precarious and Tenuous,
Two Romans.

My father was Hazardous,
Hazardous,
Dear old man,
Three Romans.

There was my brother Spurious,
Spurious Posthumous,
Spurious was spurious
Was four Romans.

My husband was Perfidious,
He was perfidious,
Five Romans.

Surreptitious, our son,
Was surreptitious,
He was six Romans.

Our cat Tedious
Still lives,

Count not Tedious
Yet.

My name is Finis,
Finis, Finis,
I am Finis,
Six, five, four, three, two,
One Roman,
Finis.

STEVIE SMITH

THE CEILING

Suppose the ceiling went outside
And then caught cold and up and died?
The only thing we'd have for proof
That he was gone, would be the roof;
I think it would be most revealing
To find out how the ceiling's feeling.

TARANTELLA

Do you remember an Inn,
Miranda?
Do you remember an Inn?
And the tedding and the spreading
Of the straw for a bedding,
And the fleas that tease in the High Pyrenees,
And the wine that tasted of the tar?
And the cheers and the jeers of the young muleteers
(Under the vine of the dark verandah)?
Do you remember an Inn, Miranda,
Do you remember an Inn?
And the cheers and the jeers of the young muleteers
Who hadn't got a penny,
And who weren't paying any,
And the hammer at the doors and the Din?
And the Hip! Hop! Hap!
Of the clap
Of the hands to the twirl and the swirl
Of the girl gone chancing,
Glancing,
Dancing,
Backing and advancing,
Snapping of a clapper to the spin
Out and in –
And the Ting, Tong, Tang of the Guitar!

Do you remember an Inn,
Miranda?
Do you remember an Inn?

HILAIRE BELLOC

IN
ARE   THIS
ONS   MIR
I   ROR
CT   I
LE   AM
REF   Guillaume   EN
AS   Apollinaire   CLOSED
NOT   AL
AND   IVE
GELS   AND
AN   REAL
INE   AS
MAG   YOU
I

TRANS. ANNE HYDE GREET

NO!

No sun – no moon!
No morn – no noon –
No dawn – no dusk – no proper time of day –
No sky – no earthly view –
No distance looking blue –
No road – no street – no 't' other side the way' –
No end to any Row –
No indications where the Crescents go –
No top to any steeple –
No recognitions of familiar people –
No courtesies for showing 'em –
No knowing 'em! –
No travelling at all – no locomotion,
No inkling of the way – no notion –
'No go' – by land or ocean –
No mail – no post –
No news from any foreign coast –
No Park – no Ring – no afternoon gentility –
No company – no nobility –
No warmth, no cheerfulness, no healthful ease,
No comfortable feel in any member –
No shade, no shine, no butterflies, no bees,
No fruits, no flowers, no leaves, no birds, –
November!

THOMAS HOOD

A TERNARIE OF LITTLES, UPON A PIPKIN OF JELLIE SENT TO A LADY

A little Saint best fits a little Shrine,
A little prop best fits a little Vine,
As my small Cruse best fits my little Wine.

A little Seed best fits a little Soyle,
A little Trade best fits a little Toyle:
As my small Jarre best fits my little Oyle.

A little Bin best fits a little Bread,
A little Garland fits a little head:
As my small stuffe best fits my little Shed.

A little Hearth best fits a little Fire,
A little Chappell fits a little Quire,
As my small Bell best fits my little Spire.

A little streame best fits a little Boat;
A little lead best fits a little Float;
As my small Pipe best fits my little note.

A little meat best fits a little bellie,
As sweetly Lady, give me leave to tell ye,
This little Pipkin fits this little Jellie.

THE CARCAJOU AND THE KINCAJOU

They tell me of a distant zoo
Where a carcajou met a kincajou.
Full soon to savage blows they came
From laughing at each other's name.
The agile ajous fought till dark
And carc slew kinc and kinc slew carc,
And beside the conquered kincajou
Lay the carcass of the carcajou.

OGDEN NASH

THE MODERN HIAWATHA

When he killed the Mudjokivis,
Of the skin he made him mittens,
Made them with the fur side inside,
Made them with the skin side outside
He, to get the warm side inside,
Put the inside skin side outside;
He, to get the cold side outside,
Put the warm side fur side inside.
That's why he put the fur side inside,
Why he put the skin side outside,
Why he turned them inside outside.

ANON.   59

THE MAD GARDENER'S SONG

He thought he saw an Elephant,
    That practised on a fife:
He looked again, and found it was
    A letter from his wife.
'At length I realise,' he said,
    'The bitterness of Life!'

He thought he saw a Buffalo
    Upon the chimney-piece:
He looked again, and found it was
    His Sister's Husband's Niece,
'Unless you leave this house,' he said,
    'I'll send for the Police!'

He thought he saw a Rattlesnake
    That questioned him in Greek:
He looked again, and found it was
    The Middle of Next Week.
'The one thing I regret,' he said,
    'Is that it cannot speak!'

He thought he saw a Banker's Clerk
    Descending from the 'bus:
He looked again, and found it was
    A Hippopotamus.

'If this should stay to dine,' he said,
  'There won't be much for us!'

He thought he saw a Kangaroo
  That worked a coffee-mill:
He looked again, and found it was
  A Vegetable-Pill.
'Were I to swallow this,' he said,
  'I should be very ill!'

He thought he saw a Coach-and-Four
  That stood beside his bed:
He looked again, and found it was
  A Bear without a Head.
'Poor thing,' he said, 'poor silly thing!
  It's waiting to be fed!'

He thought he saw an Albatross
  That fluttered round the lamp:
He looked again, and found it was
  A Penny-Postage-Stamp.
'You'd best be getting home,' he said,
  'The nights are very damp!'

He thought he saw a Garden-Door
  That opened with a key:
He looked again, and found it was

A Double Rule of Three:
'And all its mystery,' he said,
    'Is clear as day to me!'

He thought he saw an Argument
    That proved he was the Pope:
He looked again, and found it was
    A Bar of Mottled Soap.
'A fact so dread,' he faintly said,
    'Extinguishes all hope!'

LEWIS CARROLL

FROM THE EMBASSY

I, an ambassador of Otherwhere
To the unfederated states of Here and There
Enjoy (as the phrase is)
Extra-territorial privileges.
With heres and theres I seldom come to blows
Or need, as once, to sandbag all my windows.
And though the Otherwhereish currency
Cannot be quoted yet officially,
I meet less hindrance now with the exchange
Nor is my garb, even, considered strange;
And shy enquiries for literature
Come in by every post, and the side door.

THE WAIF

There lived a small hermaphrodite beside the silver
    Brent,
A stream meandering not in maps of Surrey, Bucks,
    or Kent;
Yet jealous elves from these sweet parts, this tiny mite
    to vex,
Would tease, torment, and taunt, and call him, 'Master
    Middlesex!'

He lived on acorns, dewdrops, cowslips, bilberries,
    and snow –
A small, shy, happy, tuneful thing, and innocent of woe;
Except when these malignant imps, his tenderness
    to vex,
Would tease, torment and taunt, and call him, 'Master
    Middlesex!'

He ran away; he went to sea; to far Peru he came.
There where the Ataquipa flows and odorous cinchona
    blows and no one knows his name,
He nests now with the humming-bird that sips but
    never pecks;
And silent slides the silver Brent, and mute is
    Middlesex.

WALTER DE LA MARE

WHAT THE SPIDER HEARD

Will there be time for eggnogs and eclogues
In the place where we're going?
Said the spider to the fly.

    I think not, said the fly.
    I think not, sang the chorus.
    I think not, said a stranger
    Who mysteriously happened by.

Will they beat me and treat me the way they did here,
In the place where we're going?
Asked the spider of the fly.

    It is likely, said the fly.
    Very likely, sang the chorus.
    Extremely likely, said the stranger,
    With an eager gleam in his eye.

O, why go there when we know there is nothing there
    but fear
At this place where we're going?
Said the spider to the fly.

    What a question! said the fly.
    What a question! sang the chorus.
    What a question! said the stranger,
    Leering slightly at the spider,
    Winking slyly at the fly.

THE FLY

God in His wisdom made the fly
And then forgot to tell us why.

OGDEN NASH

SPRING IN THE BRONX

Spring is sprung,
Duh grass is riz
I wonder where dem boidies is.

Duh little boids is on duh wing –
But dat's absoid:
Duh little wing is on duh boid.

A LITTLE LAMB

Mary had a little lamb,
She ate it with mint sauce,
And everywhere that Mary went
The lamb went too, of couse.

ANON.

RILLONS, RILLETTES

Rillons, *Rillettes*, they taste the same,
And would by any other name,
And are, if I may risk a joke,
Alike as two pigs in a poke.

The dishes are the same, and yet
While Tours provides the best *Rillettes*,
The best *Rillons* are made in Blois.
There must be some solution.

                                            Ah! –

Does Blois supply, do you suppose,
The best *Rillettes de Tours*, while those
Now offered by the chefs of Tours
Are, by their ancient standards, poor?

Clever, but there remains a doubt.
It is a thing to brood about,
Like non-non-A, infinity,
Or the doctrine of the Trinity.

PRIVATE MEANS IS DEAD

Private Means is dead
God rest his soul, officers and fellow-rankers said.

Captive Good, attending Captain Ill
Can tell us quite a lot about the Captain, if he will.

Major Portion
Is a disingenuous person
And as for Major Operation well I guess
We all know what his reputation is.

The crux and Colonel
Of the whole matter
(As you may read in the Journal
If it's not tattered)

Lies in the Generals Collapse Debility Panic
        and Uproar
Who are too old in any case to go to the War.

V. B. NIMBLE, V. B. QUICK

Science, Pure and Applied, by V. B. Wigglesworth, F.R.S., Quick
Professor of Biology in the University of Cambridge.
                              —a talk listed in the B.B.C.'s *Radio Times*

> V. B. Wigglesworth wakes at noon,
> Washes, shaves, and very soon
> Is at the lab; he reads his mail,
> Tweaks a tadpole by the tail,
> Undoes his coat, removes his hat,
> Dips a spider in a vat
> Of alkaline, phones the press,
> Tells them he is FRS,
> Subdivides six protocells,
> Kills a rat by ringing bells,
> Writes a treatise, edits two
> Symposia on 'Will Man Do?',
> Gives a lecture, audits three,
> Has the Sperm Club in for tea,
> Pensions off an aging spore,
> Cracks a test tube, takes some pure
> Science and applies it, finds
> His hat, adjusts it, pulls the blinds,
> Instructs the jellyfish to spawn,
> And, by one o'clock, is gone.

SQUEEZE PLAY

Jackson Pollock had a quaint
Way of saying to his sibyl,
'Shall I dribble?
Should I paint?'
And with never an instant's quibble,
Sibyl always answered,
'Dribble.'

PHYLLIS McGINLEY

IN THE DUMPS

We're all in the dumps,
For diamonds are trumps;
The kittens are gone to St Paul's!
The babies are bit,
The Moon's in a fit,
And the houses are built without walls.

ANON.

VENDETTA

An enemy of Dr Drake's,
Who, after many worse mistakes,
Prescribed him tar for stomach-aches,
    Bought four and twenty duck.
        Stowed in a sack
        On the carrier's back,
He crept next door to a tumbledown shack
    And dumped them in the muck.

They turned the doctor's head, they did;
He often now saw red, he did;
    Ev'n fees became a tax.
'That Dr Drake,' his patients said,
'There's word he's taken to his bed,
No doubt he'll very soon be dead;
    He can't endure their *Quack*(s)!'

JABBERWOCKY

'Twas brillig, and the slithy toves
    Did gyre and gimble in the wabe;
All mimsy were the borogoves,
      And the mome raths outgrabe.

'Beware the Jabberwock, my son!
    The jaws that bite, the claws that catch!
Beware the Jubjub bird and shun
      The frumious Bandersnatch!'

He took his vorpal sword in hand:
    Long time the manxome foe he sought –
So rested he by the Tumtum tree,
      And stood awhile in thought.

And as in uffish thought he stood,
    The Jabberwock, with eyes of flame,
Came whiffling through the tulgey wood,
      And burbled as it came!

One, two! One, two! And through and through
    The vorpal blade went snicker-snack!
He left it dead, and with its head
      He went galumphing back.

'And hast thou slain the Jabberwock!
    Come to my arms, my beamish boy!
O frabjous day! Callooh! Callay!'
        He chortled in his joy.

'Twas brillig and the slithy toves
    Did gyre and gimble in the wabe;
All mimsy were the borogoves,
        And the mome raths outgrabe.

LEWIS CARROLL

THE TERMITE

Some primal termite knocked on wood
And tasted it, and found it good,
And that is why your Cousin May
Fell through the parlor floor today.

Part Two: Themes

LOVE AND MARRIAGE

SYMPTOM RECITAL

I do not like my state of mind;
I'm bitter, querulous, unkind.
I hate my legs, I hate my hands,
I do not yearn for lovelier lands.
I dread the dawn's recurrent light;
I hate to go to bed at night.
I snoot at simple, earnest folk.
I cannot take the gentlest joke.
I find no peace in paint or type.
My world is but a lot of tripe.
I'm disillusioned, empty-breasted.
For what I think, I'd be arrested.
I am not sick, I am not well.
My quondam dreams are shot to hell.
My soul is crushed, my spirit sore;
I do not like me any more.
I cavil, quarrel, grumble, grouse.
I ponder on the narrow house.
I shudder at the thought of men.
I'm due to fall in love again.

FOR AN AMOROUS LADY

'Most mammals like caresses, in the sense in which we usually take the word, whereas other creatures, even tame snakes, prefer giving to receiving them.'

FROM A NATURAL-HISTORY BOOK

The pensive gnu, the staid aardvark,
Accept caresses in the dark;
The bear, equipped with paw and snout,
Would rather take than dish it out.
But snakes, both poisonous and garter,
In love are never known to barter;
The worm, though dank, is sensitive:
His noble nature bids him *give*.

But you, my dearest, have a soul
Encompassing fish, flesh, and fowl.
When amorous arts we would pursue,
You can, with pleasure, bill *or* coo.
You are, in truth, one in a million,
At once mammalian and reptilian.

TAKE ME IN YOUR ARMS, MISS MONEYPENNY-WILSON

Take me in your arms, Miss Moneypenny-Wilson,
    Take me in your arms, Miss Bates;
Fatal are your charms, Miss Moneypenny-Wilson,
    Fatal are your charms, Miss Bates;
Say you are my own, Miss Moneypenny-Wilson,
    Say you are my own, Miss Bates;
You I love alone, Miss Moneypenny-Wilson,
    You, and you alone, Miss Bates.

Sweet is the morn, Miss Moneypenny-Wilson;
    Sweet is the dawn, Miss B.,
But sweeter than the dawn and the daisies on the lawn
    Are you, sweet nymphs, to me.
Sweet, sweet, sweet is the sugar to the beet,
    Sweet is the honey to the bee,
But sweeter far than such sweets are
    Are your sweet names to me.

Deaf to my cries, Miss Moneypenny-Wilson,
    Deaf to my sighs, Miss B.,
Deaf to my songs and the story of my wrongs,
    Deaf to my minstrelsy;
Deafer than the newt to the sound of a flute,
    Deafer than a stone to the sea;

Deafer than a heifer to the sighing of a zephyr
    Are your deaf ears to me.

Cold, cold, cold as the melancholy mould,
    Cold as the foam-cold sea,
Colder than the shoulder of a neolithic boulder
    Are the shoulders you show to me.
Cruel, cruel, cruel is the flame to the fuel,
    Cruel is the axe to the tree,
But crueller and keener than a coster's concertina
    Is your cruel, cruel scorn to me.

The author loving these homely meats specially, viz.:
cream, pancakes, buttered pippin-pies (laugh, good people)
and tobacco; writ to that worthy and virtuous
gentlewoman, whom he calleth mistress, as followeth

If there were, oh! an Hellespont of cream
Between us, milk-white mistress, I would swim
To you, to show to both my love's extreme,
Leander-like, – yea! dive from brim to brim.
But met I with a buttered pippin-pie
Floating upon 't, that would I make my boat
To waft me to you without jeopardy,
Though sea-sick I might be while it did float.
Yet if a storm should rise, by night or day,
Of sugar-snows and hail of caraways,
Then, if I found a pancake in my way,
It like a plank should bring me to your kays;
    Which having found, if they tobacco kept,
    The smoke should dry me well before I slept.

On sunny days there in the shade
Beneath the trees reclined a maid
Who lifted up her dress (she said)
To keep the moonbeams off her head.

*

The impudence of some people,
To say such things about an honest woman!
'Stop thief!' cries the burglar,
And carries on breaking in.

*

While describing to her best friend
Her adventures with her lover,
She realized she was talking to her husband,
And added, 'And then I woke up.'

BHARTṚHARI
TRANS. JOHN BROUGH

He marvelled at her breasts, and when he'd seen them
He shook his head, to disengage his gaze
Trapped in between them.

80   AMARU
TRANS. JOHN BROUGH

ALICE IS AT IT AGAIN

In a dear little village remote and obscure
A beautiful maiden resided,
As to whether or not her intentions were pure
Opinion was sharply divided.
She loved to lie out 'neath the darkening sky
And allow the soft breeze to entrance her,
She whispered her dreams to the birds flying by
But seldom received any answer.

Over the field and along the lane
Gentle Alice would love to stray,
When it came to the end of the day,
She would wander away unheeding,
Dreaming her innocent dreams she strolled
Quite unaffected by heat or cold,
Frequently freckled or soaked with rain,
Alice was out in the lane.
Whom she met there
Every day there
Was a question answered by none,
But she'd get there
And she'd stay there
Till whatever she did was undoubtedly done.
Over the field and along the lane
When her parents had called in vain,

Sadly, sorrowfully, they'd complain,
'Alice is at it again.'

Though that dear little village
Surrounded by trees
Had neither a school nor a college,
Gentle Alice acquired from the birds and the bees
Some exceedingly practical knowledge.
The curious secrets that nature revealed
She refused to allow to upset her
But she thought when observing the beasts of the field
That things might have been organized better.

Over the field and along the lane
Gentle Alice one summer's day
Met a man who was driving a dray
And he whisked her away to London.
Then, after many a year had passed,
Alice returned to her home at last
Wearing some pearls and a velvet train,
Bearing a case of champagne.
They received her
Fairly coldly
But when wine had lifted the blight
They believed her
When she boldly
Said the Salvation Army had shown her the light.

When she had left by the evening train
Both her parents in grief and pain
Murmured brokenly, 'More champagne –
Alice is at it again!'

Over the field and along the lane
Gentle Alice would make up
And take up – her stand.
The road was not exactly arterial
But it led to a town near by
Where quite a lot of masculine material
Caught her roving eye.
She was ready to hitchhike
Cadillac or motor-bike,
She wasn't proud or choosey,
All she
Was aiming to be
Was a prinked up,
Minked up
Fly-by-night Floosie.
When old Rajahs
Gave her pearls as large as
Nuts on a chestnut tree
All she said was, 'Fiddlededee,
The wages of sin will be the death of me!'

Over the field and along the lane
Gentle Alice's parents would wait hand in hand.
Her dear old white-headed mother wistfully sipping
    champagne
Said, 'We've spoiled our child – spared the rod,
Open up the caviar and say Thank God,
We've got no cause to complain,
Alice is at it,
Alice is at it,
Alice is at it again.'

NOËL COWARD

A TRUE MAID

No, no; for my virginity,
    When I lose that, says Rose, I'll die;
Behind the elms, last night, cried Dick,
    Rose, were you not extremely sick?

A SONG OF A YOUNG LADY
TO HER ANCIENT LOVER

Ancient Person, for whom I
All the flatt'ring Youth defie;
Long be it ere thou grow Old,
Aking, shaking, crasie, cold.
But still continue as thou art,
Ancient Person of my Heart.

On thy wither'd Lips and dry,
Which like barren Furrows lye,
Brooding Kisses I will pour,
Shall thy youthful Heat restore.
Such kind Show'rs in Autumn fall,
And a second Spring recall:
Nor from thee will ever part,
Ancient Person of My Heart.

Thy Nobler Parts, which but to name,
In our Sex would be counted Shame,
By Age's frozen Grasp possess'd,
From their Ice shall be releas'd:
And, sooth'd by my reviving Hand,
In former Warmth and Vigour stand.
All a Lover's Wish can reach,
For thy Joy my Love shall teach:

And for thy Pleasure shall improve
All that Art can add to Love.
Yet still I love thee without Art,
Ancient Person of My Heart.

THE OLD MAN'S COMPLAINT:
BY MR WELLS

Ah, pity Love where e'r it grows!
See how in me it overflows,
In dripping Eyes and dropping Nose.

So strange a thing is seldom seen;
My Age is dull, my Love is keen;
Above I'm grey, but elsewhere green.

Aloof, perhaps I court and prate;
But something near I would be at,
Tho' I'm so old I scarce know what.

ALWAYS TRUE TO YOU IN MY FASHION

Oh, Bill,
Why can't you behave,
Why can't you behave?
How in hell can you be jealous
When you know, baby, I'm your slave?
I'm just mad for you,
And I'll always be,
But naturally

If a custom-tailored vet
Asks me out for something wet,
When the vet begins to pet, I cry 'Hooray!'
But I'm always true to you, darlin', in my fashion,
Yes, I'm always true to you, darlin', in my way.
I enjoy a tender pass
By the boss of Boston, Mass.,
Though his pass is middle-class and notta Backa Bay.
But I'm always true to you, darlin', in my fashion,
Yes, I'm always true to you, darlin', in my way.
There's a madman known as Mack
Who is planning to attack,
If his mad attack means a Cadillac, okay!
But I'm always true to you, darlin', in my fashion,
Yes, I'm always true to you, darlin', in my way.

I've been asked to have a meal
By a big tycoon in steel,
If the meal includes a deal, accept I may.
But I'm always true to you, darlin', in my fashion,
Yes, I'm always true to you, darlin', in my way.
I could never curl my lip
To a dazzlin' diamond clip,
Though the clip meant 'let 'er rip,' I'd not say 'Nay!'
But I'm always true to you, darlin', in my fashion,
Yes, I'm always true to you, darlin', in my way.
There's an oil man known as Tex
Who is keen to give me checks,
And his checks, I fear, mean that sex is here to stay!
But I'm always true to you, darlin', in my fashion,
Yes, I'm always true to you, darlin', in my way.

There's a wealthy Hindu priest
Who's a wolf, to say the least,
When the priest goes too far east, I also stray.
But I'm always true to you, darlin', in my fashion,
Yes, I'm always true to you, darlin', in my way.
There's a lush from Portland, Ore.,
Who is rich but such a bore,
When the bore falls on the floor, I let him lay.
But I'm always true to you, darlin', in my fashion,

Yes, I'm always true to you, darlin', in my way.
Mister Harris, plutocrat,
Wants to give my cheek a pat,
If the Harris pat
Means a Paris hat,
Bébé, Oo-la-la!
Mais je suis toujours fidèle, darlin', in my fashion,
Oui, je suis toujours fidèle, darlin', in my way.

From Ohio Mister Thorne
Calls me up from night 'til morn,
Mister Thorne once cornered corn and that ain't hay.
But I'm always true to you, darlin', in my fashion,
Yes, I'm always true to you, darlin', in my way.
From Milwaukee, Mister Fritz
Often moves me to the Ritz,
Mister Fritz is full of Schlitz and full of play.
But I'm always true to you, darlin', in my fashion,
Yes, I'm always true to you, darlin', in my way.
Mister Gable, I mean Clark,
Wants me on his boat to park,
If the Gable boat
Means a sable coat,
Anchors aweigh!
But I'm always true to you, darlin', in my fashion,
Yes, I'm always true to you, darlin', in my way.

LOVE ME LITTLE, LOVE ME LONG

You say, to me-wards your affection's strong;
Pray love me little, so you love me long.
Slowly goes farre: The meane is best: Desire
Grown violent, do's either die, or tire.

ROBERT HERRICK

ELINOR GLYN

Would you like to sin
with Elinor Glyn
on a tiger-skin?
Or would you prefer
to err
with her
on some other fur?

ANON.

FATAL LOVE

Poor Hal caught his death standing under a spout,
Expecting till midnight when Nan would come out,
But fatal his patience, as cruel the dame,
And curs'd was the weather that quench'd the
     man's flame.

Whoe'er thou art, that read'st these moral lines,
Make love at home, and go to bed betimes.

ONE PERFECT ROSE

A single flow'r he sent me, since we met.
All tenderly his messenger he chose;
Deep-hearted, pure, with scented dew still wet –
One perfect rose.

I knew the language of the floweret;
'My fragile leaves,' it said, 'his heart enclose.'
Love long has taken for his amulet
One perfect rose.

Why is it no one ever sent me yet
One perfect limousine, do you suppose?
Ah no, it's always just my luck to get
One perfect rose.

ICH LIEBE SOLCHE WEISSE GLIEDER

I love this white and slender body,
    These limbs that answer love's caresses,
Passionate eyes, and forehead covered
    With a wave of thick, black tresses.

You are the very one I've searched for
    In many lands, in every weather.
You are my sort; you understand me;
    As equals we can talk together.

In me you've found the man you care for.
    And, for a while, you'll richly pay me
With kindness, kisses, and endearments –
    And then, as usual, you'll betray me.

ENDING

The love we thought would never stop
now cools like a congealing chop.
The kisses that were hot as curry
are bird-pecks taken in a hurry.
The hands that held electric charges
now lie inert as four moored barges.
The feet that ran to meet a date
are running slow and running late.
The eyes that shone and seldom shut
are victims of a power cut.
The parts that then transmitted joy
are now reserved and cold and coy.
Romance, expected once to stay,
has left a note saying GONE AWAY.

THE TROUBLE WITH WOMEN IS MEN

A husband is a man who two minutes after his head
      touches the pillow is snoring like an overloaded
      omnibus,
Particularly on those occasions when between the
      humidity and the mosquitoes your own bed is no
      longer a bed, but an insomnibus,
And if you turn on the light for a little reading he is
      sensitive to the faintest gleam,
But if by any chance you are asleep and he wakeful, he
      is not slow to rouse you with the complaint that
      he can't close his eyes, what about slipping
      downstairs and freezing him a cooling dish of
      pistachio ice cream.
His touch with a bottle opener is sure,
But he cannot help you get a tight dress over your head
      without catching three hooks and a button in your
      coiffure.
Nor can he so much as wash his ears without leaving
      an inch of water on the bathroom linoleum,
But if you mention it you evoke not a promise to splash
      no more but a mood of deep melancholium.
Indeed, each time he transgresses your chance of
      correcting his faults grows lesser,
Because he produces either a maddeningly logical
      explanation or a look of martyrdom which leaves

you instead of him feeling the remorse of the
transgressor.
Such are husbandly foibles, but there are moments
when a foible ceases to be a foible.
Next time you ask for a glass of water and when he
brings it you have a needle almost threaded and
instead of setting it down he stands there holding
it out to you, just kick him fairly hard in the
stomach, you will find it thoroughly enjoible.

A WORD TO HUSBANDS

To keep your marriage brimming,
With love in the loving cup,
Whenever you're wrong, admit it;
Whenever you're right, shut up.

OGDEN NASH

AUTUMN

He told his life story to Mrs Courtly
Who was a widow. 'Let us get married shortly',
He said. 'I am no longer passionate,
But we can have some conversation before it is
    too late.'

ST IVES

As I was going to St Ives
I met a man with seven wives.
Said he, 'I think it's much more fun
Than getting stuck with only one.'

HOT AND COLD

A woman who my mother knows
Came in and took off all her clothes.

Said I, not being very old,
'By golly gosh, you must be cold!'

'No, no!' she cried. 'Indeed I'm not!
I'm feeling devilishly hot!'

THE MISTAKE

He left his pants upon a chair:
She was a widow, so she said:
But he was apprehended, bare,
By one who rose up from the dead.

SUCKING CIDER
THROUGH A STRAW

The prettiest girl
That ever I saw,
Was sucking cider
Through a straw.

I told that girl
I didn't see how
She sucked the cider
Through a straw.

And cheek by cheek
And jaw by jaw
We sucked that cider
Through that straw.

And all at once
That straw did slip;
I sucked some cider
From her lip.

And now I've got
Me a mother-in-law
From sucking cider
Through a straw.

ANON.

THE NEWLYWEDS

*After a one-day honeymoon, the Fishers rushed off to a soft
drink bottlers' convention, then on to a ball game, a TV
rehearsal and a movie preview.*   *— Life*

'We're married,' said Eddie.
Said Debbie, 'Incredi-

ble! When is our honey-
moon?' 'Over and done,' he

replied. 'Feeling logy?
Drink Coke.' 'Look at Yogi

go!' Debbie cried. 'Groovy!'
'Rehearsal?' 'The movie.'

'Some weddie,' said Debbie.
Said Eddie, 'Yeah, mebbe.'

ON KANT'S DEFINITION OF MARRIAGE
IN *THE METAPHYSICS OF ETHICS*

That pact for reciprocity in use
Of sexual organs and worldly possessions
Which marriage meant for him, in my submission
Urgently needs securing from abuse.

I gather certain partners have defaulted.
Allegedly the organs acting for them
Vanished when they decided to withdraw them.
Loopholes were found: something that must be halted.

Recourse to law would seem the only way
To get those organs duly confiscated.
Perhaps each partner then can be persuaded

To check again on what the contracts say.
If he won't do so, someone's sure to send
The bailiffs in – a most unhappy end.

SOME PAINS
AND PLEASURES

SPECTATOR AB EXTRA

As I sat at the Café I said to myself,
They may talk as they please about what they call pelf,
They may sneer as they like about eating and drinking,
But help it I cannot, I cannot help thinking
   How pleasant it is to have money, heigh-ho!
   How pleasant it is to have money.

I sit at my table *en grand seigneur,*
And when I have done, throw a crust to the poor;
Not only the pleasure itself of good living,
But also the pleasure of now and then giving:
   So pleasant it is to have money, heigh-ho!
   So pleasant it is to have money.

They may talk as they please about what they call pelf,
And how one ought never to think of one's self,
How pleasures of thought surpass eating and
     drinking –
My pleasure of thought is the pleasure of thinking
   How pleasant it is to have money, heigh-ho!
   How pleasant it is to have money.

RECIPE FOR A SALAD

To make this condiment, your poet begs
The pounded yellow of two hard-boiled eggs;
Two boiled potatoes, passed through kitchen-sieve,
Smoothness and softness to the salad give;
Let onion atoms lurk within the bowl,
And, half-suspected, animate the whole.
Of mordant mustard add a single spoon,
Distrust the condiment that bites so soon;
But deem it not, thou man of herbs, a fault,
To add a double quantity of salt.
And, lastly, o'er the flavored compound toss
A magic soup-spoon of anchovy sauce.
Oh, green and glorious! Oh, herbaceous treat!
'T would tempt the dying anchorite to eat;
Back to the world he'd turn his fleeting soul,
And plunge his fingers in the salad bowl!
Serenely full, the epicure would say,
Fate can not harm me, I have dined to-day!

PEAS

I always eat peas with honey,
I've done it all my life,
They do taste kind of funny,
But it keeps them on the knife.

ANON.

THE BUN

The muffin and the crumpet are
 When adequately done
A dish to make a curate wish
 To excel in feats of fun;
A Canon booms, 'tis said, when fed
 On toasted Sallie Lunn;
E'en Deans, I ween, plum cake being seen,
 Have been observed to run:
But, Ah! a Bishop come to tea!
 He takes the Bun.

WALTER DE LA MARE

SONNET TO VAUXHALL

The cold transparent ham is on my fork –
   It hardly rains – and hark the bell! – ding-dingle –
Away! Three thousand feet at gravel work,
   Mocking a Vauxhall shower! – Married and Single
Crush – rush; – Soak'd Silks with wet white
     Satin mingle.
   Hengler! Madame! round whom all bright
     sparks lurk,
Calls audibly on Mr and Mrs Pringle
   To study the Sublime, &c. – (vide Burke)
All Noses are upturn'd! – Whish – ish! – On high
   The rocket rushes – trails – just steals in sight –
Then droops and melts in bubbles of blue light –
   And Darkness reigns – Then balls flare up and die –
Wheels whiz – smack crackers – serpents twist –
     and then
   Back to the cold transparent ham again!

SMELT AND TASTED

The nose and palate never doubt
Their verdicts on the world without,
But instantaneously condemn
Or praise each fact that reaches them:
Our tastes may change in time, it's true,
But for the fairer if they do.

Compared with almost any brute,
Our savouring is less acute,
But, subtly as they judge, no beast
Can solve the mystery of a feast,
Where love is strengthened, hope restored,
In hearts by chemical accord.

W. H. AUDEN

HEARD AND SEEN

Events reported by the ear
Are soft or loud, not far or near,
In what is heard we only sense
Transition and impermanence:
A bark, a laugh, a rifle-shot,
These may concern us or may not.

What-has-been and what-is-to-be
To vision form a unity:
The seen hill stays the way it is,
But forecasts greater distances,
And we acknowledge with delight
A so-on after every sight.

THE 'SATIRE'

The dying man on his pillow
    Turned slowly his head.
'Five years on my Satire on Man
    I spent,' he said.
'But, lying alone, I have mused
    On myself, of late!'

Smiling, he nodded; and glanced
    At the ash in the grate.

WALTER DE LA MARE

THE COMMING OF GOOD LUCK

So Good-luck came, and on my roofe did light,
Like noyse-lesse Snow; or as the dew of night:
Not all at once, but gently, as the trees
Are, by the Sun-beams, tickel'd by degrees.

ROBERT HERRICK

BLISSE

All Blisse
Consists in this,
To do as Adam did:
And not to know those Superficial Toys
Which in the Garden once were hid.
Those little new Invented Things,
Cups, Saddles, Crowns are Childish Joys
So Ribbans are and Rings,
Which all our Happiness destroys.

Nor God
In his Abode
Not Saints nor little Boys
Nor Angels made them: only foolish Men,
Grown mad with Custom on those Toys
Which more increas their Wants do dote,
And when they Older are do then
Those Bables chiefly note
With Greedier Eys, more Boys tho Men.

DIVIDED DESTINIES

It was an artless *Bandar* and he danced upon a pine,
And much I wondered how he lived, and where the
    beast might dine,
And many many other things, till, o'er my morning
    smoke,
I slept the sleep of idleness and dreamt that
    Bandar spoke.

He said:– 'Oh man of many clothes! Sad crawler on
    the Hills!
'Observe, I know not Ranken's shop, nor Ranken's
    monthly bills!
'I take no heed to trousers or the coats that you call
    dress;
'Nor am I plagued with little cards for little drinks
    at Mess.

'I steal the bunnia's grain at morn, at noon and
    eventide
'(For he is fat and I am spare), I roam the
    mountain-side.
'I follow no man's carriage, and no, never in my life
'Have I flirted at Peliti's with another *Bandar's* wife.

'O man of futile fopperies – unnecessary wraps;
'I own no ponies in the hills, I drive no tallwheeled
     traps.
'I buy me not twelve-button gloves, "short-sixes" eke,
     or rings,
'Nor do I waste at Hamilton's my wealth on
     "pretty things".

'I quarrel with my wife at home, we never fight abroad;
'But Mrs B. has grasped the fact I *am* her only lord.
'I never heard of fever – dumps nor debts depress
     my soul;
'And I pity and despise you!' Here he pouched my
     breakfast-roll.

His hide was very mangy and his face was very red,
And ever and anon he scratched with energy his head.
His manners were not always nice, but how my
     spirit cried
To be an artless *Bandar* loose upon the mountain-side!

LOOK FOR THE SILVER LINING

I can't say that I feel particularly one way or the other
    towards bell-boys,
But I do admit that I haven't much use for the it's-just-
    as-well boys,
The cheery souls who drop around after every
    catastrophe and think they are taking the curse off
By telling you about somebody who is even worse off.
No matter how deep and dark your pit, how dank your
    shroud,
Their heads are heroically unbloody and unbowed.
If you have just lost the one love of your life, there is no
    possible doubt of it,
They tell you there are as good fish in the sea as ever
    came out of it.
If you are fined ten dollars for running past a light
    when you didn't but the cop says you did,
They say Cheer up think of the thousand times you ran
    past them and didn't get caught so you're really
    ten thousand bucks ahead. Hey old kid?
If you lose your job they tell you how lucky you are
    that you've saved up a little wealth
And then when the bank folds with the savings they
    tell you you sure are lucky to still have your
    health.
Life to them is just one long happy game,

At the conclusion of which the One Great Scorer
        writes not whether you won it or lost it, but how
        you played it, against your name.
Kismet, they say, it's Fate. What is to be, will be.
        Buck up! Take heart!
Kismet indeed! Nobody can make me grateful for Paris
        Green in the soup just by assuring me that it
        comes that way Allah carte.

OGDEN NASH

HOTEL

My room's shaped like a cage the sun
Puts his arm right through the window
But I who wish to smoke and dream
Use it to light my cigarette
I don't want to work I want to smoke

PRAISE IS A MIRROR

Praise is a mirror that flatters the mind,
    That tells us of goodness, and virtues, and graces;
As that on our toilet instructs us to find
    The dimples and smiles which appear on our faces;
To which our attention we cannot refrain,
    Though we draw off confus'd, yet but see its
        attraction,
In spite of ourselves we return back again,
    Regard, are abus'd, and yet feel satisfaction.

I know I'm deceiv'd, and I say to my heart,
    You believe that sincere which is nought but
        profusion:
Call pleasure what soon will severe make you smart,
    And hug that for a substance you'll find but
        delusion.
Your praises are flatt'ry, I know it as plain
    As if you had said, 'I am false, and deceive you':
But truth, reason, every thing, argues in vain;
    For such is my weakness, I blush and believe you.

THE NIGHTMARE

When you're lying awake with a dismal headache, and
    repose is taboo'd by anxiety,
I conceive you may use any language you choose to
    indulge in, without impropriety;
For your brain is on fire – the bedclothes conspire of
    usual slumber to plunder you:
First your counterpane goes, and uncovers your toes,
    and your sheet slips demurely from under you;
Then the blanketing tickles – you feel like mixed
    pickles – so terribly sharp is the pricking,
And you're hot, and you're cross, and you tumble and
    toss till there's nothing 'twixt you and the ticking.
Then the bedclothes all creep to the ground in a heap,
    and you pick 'em all up in a tangle;
Next your pillow resigns and politely declines to
    remain at its usual angle!
Well, you get some repose in the form of a doze, with
    hot eye-balls and head ever aching,
But your slumbering teems with such horrible dreams
    that you'd very much better be waking;
For you dream you are crossing the Channel, and
    tossing about in a steamer from Harwich –
Which is something between a large bathing machine
    and a very small second-class carriage –

And you're giving a treat (penny ice and cold meat) to
     a party of friends and relations –
They're a ravenous horde – and they all came on board
     at Sloane Square and South Kensington Stations.
And bound on that journey you find your attorney
     (who started that morning from Devon);
He's a bit undersized, and you don't feel surprised
     when he tells you he's only eleven.
Well, you're driving like mad with this singular lad
     (by-the-bye the ship's now a four-wheeler),
And you're playing round games, and he calls you bad
     names when you tell him that 'ties pay the dealer';
But this you can't stand, so you throw up your hand,
     and you find you're as cold as an icicle,
In your shirt and your socks (the black silk with gold
     clocks), crossing Salisbury Plain on a bicycle:
And he and the crew are on bicycles too – which
     they've somehow or other invested in –
And he's telling the tars, all the particu*lars* of a
     company he's interested in –
It's a scheme of devices, to get at low prices, all goods
     from cough mixtures to cables
(Which tickled the sailors) by treating retailers, as
     though they were all vege*t*ables –

You get a good spadesman to plant a small tradesman,
    (first take off his boots with a boot-tree),
And his legs will take root, and his fingers will shoot,
    and they'll blossom and bud like a fruit-tree –
From the greengrocer tree you get grapes and green
    pea, cauliflower, pineapple, and cranberries,
While the pastrycook plant, cherry brandy will grant,
    apple puffs, and three-corners, and banberries –
The shares are a penny, and ever so many are taken by
    Rothschild and Baring,
And just as a few are allotted to you, you awake with a
    shudder despairing –
You're a regular wreck, with a crick in your neck, and
    no wonder you snore, for your head's on the floor,
    and you've needles and pins from your soles to
    your shins, and your flesh is a-creep for your left
    leg's asleep, and you've cramp in your toes, and a
    fly on your nose, and some fluff in your lung, and a
    feverish tongue, and a thirst that's intense, and a
    general sense that you haven't been sleeping in
    clover;
But the darkness has passed, and it's daylight at last,
    and the night has been long – ditto ditto my
    song – and thank goodness they're both of them
    over!

COMPLAINT TO FOUR ANGELS

Every night at sleepy-time
Into bed I gladly climb.
Every night anew I hope
That with the covers I can cope.

Adjust the blanket fore and aft.
Swallow next a soothing draught;
Then a page of Scott or Cooper
May induce a healthful stupor.

Oh the soft luxurious darkness,
Fit for Morgan, or for Harkness!
Traffic dies along the street.
The light is out. So are your feet.

Adjust the blanket aft and fore,
Sigh, and settle down once more.
Behold, a breeze! The curtains puff.
One blanket isn't quite enough.

Yawn and rise and seek your slippers,
Which, by now, are cold as kippers.
Yawn, and stretch, and prod yourself,
And fetch a blanket from the shelf.

And so to bed again, again,
Cozy under blankets twain.
Welcome warmth and sweet nirvana
Till eight o'clock or so mañana.

You sleep as deep as Keats or Bacon;
Then you dream and toss and waken.
Where is the breeze? There isn't any.
Two blankets, boy, are one too many.

O stilly night, why are you not
Consistent in your cold and hot?
O slumber's chains, unlocked so oft
With blankets being donned or doffed!

The angels who should guard my bed
I fear are slumbering instead.
O angels, please resume your hovering;
I'll sleep, and you adjust the covering.

EPIGRAM V.9

A slight cold or a touch of flu,
but when THE SPECIALIST and all his crew
of a hundred students once are through,
and every inch of me's been handled twice
by a hundred medics' hands as cold as ice,
the pneumonia I didn't have I DO!

MARTIAL
TRANS. TONY HARRISON

EPIGRAM IV.70

When Ammianus' father breathed
His last, his son, hovering in hope,
Found that the final will bequeathed
Him nothing but a length of rope.
Though none of us dreamed he could regret
The old man's death, he's most upset.

MARTIAL
TRANS. JAMES MICHIE

I'VE BEEN TO A MARVELLOUS PARTY

Quite for no reason
I'm here for the Season
And high as a kite,
Living in error
With Maud at Cap Ferrat
Which couldn't be right.
Everyone's here and frightfully gay,
Nobody cares what people say,
Though the Riviera
Seems really much queerer
Than Rome at its height,
Yesterday night –

I've been to a marvellous party
With Nounou and Nada and Nell,
It was in the fresh air
And we went as we were
And we stayed as we were
Which was Hell.
Poor Grace started singing at midnight
And didn't stop singing till four;
We knew the excitement was bound to begin
When Laura got blind on Dubonnet and gin
And scratched her veneer with a Cartier pin,
I couldn't have liked it more.

I've been to a marvellous party,
I must say the fun was intense,
We all had to do
What the people we knew
Would be doing a hundred years hence.
Dear Cecil arrived wearing armour,
Some shells and a black feather boa,
Poor Millicent wore a surrealist comb
Made of bits of mosaic from St Peter's in Rome,
But the weight was so great that she had to go home,
I couldn't have liked it more!

People's behaviour
Away from Belgravia
Would make you aghast,
So much variety
Watching Society
Scampering past,
If you have any mind at all
Gibbon's divine *Decline and Fall*
Seems pretty flimsy,
No more than a whimsy,
By way of contrast
On Saturday last –

I've been to a marvellous party,
We didn't start dinner till ten
And young Bobbie Carr
Did a stunt at the bar
With a lot of extraordinary men;
Dear Baba arrived with a turtle
Which shattered us all to the core,
The Grand Duke was dancing a foxtrot with me
When suddenly Cyril screamed Fiddledidee
And ripped off his trousers and jumped in the sea,
I couldn't have liked it more.

I've been to a marvellous party,
Elise made an entrance with May,
You'd never have guessed
From her fisherman's vest
That her bust had been whittled away.
Poor Lulu got fried on Chianti
And talked about esprit de corps.
Maurice made a couple of passes at Gus
And Freddie, who hates any kind of a fuss,
Did half the Big Apple and twisted his truss,
I couldn't have liked it more.

I've been to a marvellous party,
We played the most wonderful game,
Maureen disappeared

And came back in a beard
And we all had to guess at her name!
We talked about growing old gracefully
And Elsie who's seventy-four
Said, 'A, it's a question of being sincere,
And B, if you're supple you've nothing to fear.'
Then she swung upside down from a glass chandelier,
I couldn't have liked it more.

THE PARTY NEXT DOOR

I trust I am not a spoilsport, but there is one thing
    I deplore,
And that is a party next door.
I am by nature very fond of everybody, even my
    neighbors,
And I think it only right that they should enjoy some
    kind of diversion after their labors,
But why don't they get their diversion by going to the
    movies or the Little Theater or the Comédie
    Française or the Commedia dell'arte?
Why do they always have to be giving a party?
You may think you have heard a noise because you have
    heard an artillery barrage or an avalanche or the
    subway's horrendous roar,
But you have never really heard anything until you
    have heard a party next door.
At a party next door the guests stampede like
    elephants in wooden shoes and gallop like
    desperate polo players,
And all the women are coloratura sopranos and all the
    men are train announcers and hogcallers and
    saxophone solo players.
They all have screamingly funny stories to tell to each
    other,

And half of them get at one end of the house and half of
 them get at the other end of the yard and then
 they yell to each other,
And even if the patrolman looks in from his beat they
 do not moderate or stop,
No, they just seduce the cop.
And at last you manage to doze off by the dawn's early
 light,
And they wake you up all over again shouting good
 night,
And whether it consists of two quiet old ladies
 dropping in for a game of bridge or a lot of
 revelers getting really sort of out-of-bounds-like,
That's what a party next door always sounds like,
So when you see somebody with a hoarse voice and a
 pallid face and eyes bleary and red-rimmed and
 sore,
It doesn't mean they've been on a party themselves, no,
 it probably means that they have experienced a
 party next door.

EVENING MUSICALE

Candles. Red tulips, ninety cents the bunch.
   Two lions, Grade B. A newly tuned piano.
No cocktails, but a dubious kind of punch,
   Lukewarm and weak. A harp and a soprano.
The 'Lullaby' of Brahms. Somebody's cousin
   From Forest Hills, addicted to the pun.
Two dozen gentlemen; ladies, three dozen,
   Earringed and powdered. Sandwiches at one.

The ash trays few, the ventilation meager.
   Shushes to greet the late-arriving guest
Or quell the punch-bowl group. A young man eager
   To render 'Danny Deever' by request.
And sixty people trying to relax
On little rented chairs with gilded backs.

STATELY AS A GALLEON

My neighbour, Mrs Fanshaw, is portly-plump and gay,
She must be over sixty-seven, if she is a day.
You might have thought her life was dull,
It's one long whirl instead.
I asked her all about it, and this is what she said:

I've joined an Olde Thyme Dance Club, the trouble
    is that there
Are too many ladies over, and no gentlemen to spare.
It seems a shame, it's not the same,
But still it has to be,
Some ladies have to dance together,
One of them is me.

Stately as a galleon, I sail across the floor,
Doing the Military Two-step, as in the days of yore.
I dance with Mrs Tiverton; she's light on her feet,
    in spite
Of turning the scale at fourteen stone, and being
    of medium height.
So gay the band,
So giddy the sight,
Full evening dress is a must,
But the zest goes out of a beautiful waltz
When you dance it bust to bust.

So, stately as two galleons, we sail across the floor,
Doing the Valse Valeta as in the days of yore.
The gent is Mrs Tiverton, I am her lady fair,
She bows to me ever so nicely and I curtsey to her
     with care.
So gay the band,
So giddy the sight,
But it's not the same in the end
For a lady is never a gentleman, though
She may be your bosom friend.

So, stately as a galleon, I sail across the floor,
Doing the dear old Lancers, as in the days of yore.
I'm led by Mrs Tiverton, she swings me round
     and round
And though she manoeuvres me wonderfully well
I never get off the ground.
So gay the band,
So giddy the sight,
I try not to get depressed.
And it's done me a power of good to explode,
And get this lot off my chest.

A LITERARY DINNER

Come here, said my hostess, her face making room
for one of those pink introductory smiles
that link, like a valley of fruit trees in bloom,
the slopes of two names.
I want you, she murmured, to eat Dr James.

I was hungry. The Doctor looked good. He had read
the great book of the week and had liked it, he said,
because it was powerful. So I was brought
a generous helping. His mauve-bosomed wife
kept showing me, very politely, I thought,
the tenderest bits with the point of her knife.
I ate – and in Egypt the sunsets were swell;
The Russians were doing remarkably well;
Had I met a Prince Poprinsky, whom he had known
in Caparabella, or was it Mentone?
They had travelled extensively, he and his wife;
her hobby was People, his hobby was Life.
All was good and well cooked, but the tastiest part
was his nut-flavored, crisp cerebellum. The heart
resembled a shiny brown date,
and I stowed all the studs on the edge of my plate.

VERS DE SOCIÉTÉ

My wife and I have asked a crowd of craps
To come and waste their time and ours: perhaps
You'd care to join us? In a pig's arse, friend.
Day comes to an end.
The gas fire breathes, the trees are darkly swayed.
And so *Dear Warlock-Williams: I'm afraid* —

Funny how hard it is to be alone.
I could spend half my evenings, if I wanted,
Holding a glass of washing sherry, canted
Over to catch the drivel of some bitch
Who's read nothing but *Which*;
Just think of all the spare time that has flown

Straight into nothingness by being filled
With forks and faces, rather than repaid
Under a lamp, hearing the noise of wind,
And looking out to see the moon thinned
To an air-sharpened blade.
A life, and yet how sternly it's instilled

All solitude is selfish. No one now
Believes the hermit with his gown and dish
Talking to God (who's gone too); the big wish
Is to have people nice to you, which means

Doing it back somehow.
Virtue is social. Are, then, these routines

Playing at goodness, like going to church?
Something that bores us, something we don't do well
(Asking that ass about his fool research)
But try to feel, because, however crudely,
It shows us what should be?
Too subtle, that. Too decent, too. Oh hell,

Only the young can be alone freely.
The time is shorter now for company,
And sitting by a lamp more often brings
Not peace, but other things.
Beyond the light stand failure and remorse
Whispering *Dear Warlock-Williams: Why, of course* —

CHARACTERS

HOW PLEASANT TO KNOW MR LEAR

'How pleasant to know Mr Lear!'
   Who has written such volumes of stuff!
Some think him ill-tempered and queer,
   But a few think him pleasant enough.

His mind is concrete and fastidious,
   His nose is remarkably big;
His visage is more or less hideous,
   His beard it resembles a wig.

He has ears, and two eyes, and ten fingers,
   Leastways if you reckon two thumbs;
Long ago he was one of the singers,
   But now he is one of the dumbs.

He sits in a beautiful parlour,
   With hundreds of books on the wall;
He drinks a great deal of Marsala,
   But never gets tipsy at all.

He has many friends, laymen and clerical,
   Old Foss is the name of his cat:
His body is perfectly spherical,
   He weareth a runcible hat.

When he walks in a waterproof white,
    The children run after him so!
Calling out, 'He's come out in his night-
    gown, that crazy old Englishman, oh!'

He weeps by the side of the ocean,
    He weeps on the top of the hill;
He purchases pancakes and lotion,
    And chocolate shrimps from the mill.

He reads but he cannot speak Spanish,
    He cannot abide ginger-beer:
Ere the days of his pilgrimage vanish,
    How pleasant to know Mr Lear!

POSTERITY

Jake Balokowsky, my biographer,
Has this page microfilmed. Sitting inside
His air-conditioned cell at Kennedy
In jeans and sneakers, he's no call to hide
Some slight impatience with his destiny:
'I'm stuck with this old fart at least a year;

I wanted to teach school in Tel Aviv,
But Myra's folks' – he makes the money sign –
'Insisted I got tenure. When there's kids –'
He shrugs. 'It's stinking dead, the research line;
Just let me put this bastard on the skids,
I'll get a couple of semesters leave

To work on Protest Theater.' They both rise,
Make for the Coke dispenser. 'What's he like?
Christ, I just told you. Oh, you know the thing,
That crummy textbook stuff from Freshman Psych,
Not out of kicks or something happening –
One of those old-type *natural* fouled-up guys.'

HENRY KING

Who chewed bits of string, and was early cut off in dreadful agonies

The Chief Defect of Henry King
    Was chewing little bits of String.
At last he swallowed some which tied
    Itself in ugly Knots inside.
Physicians of the Utmost Fame
Were called at once; but when they came
They answered, as they took their Fees,
'There is no Cure for this Disease.
Henry will very soon be dead.'
His Parents stood about his Bed
Lamenting his Untimely Death,
When Henry, with his Latest Breath,
Cried – 'Oh, my Friends, be warned by me,
That Breakfast, Dinner, Lunch, and Tea
Are all the Human Frame requires . . .'
With that, the Wretched Child expires.

THE PURIST

I give you now Professor Twist,
A conscientious scientist.
Trustees exclaimed, 'He never bungles!'
And sent him off to distant jungles.
Camped on a tropic riverside,
One day he missed his loving bride.
She had, the guide informed him later,
Been eaten by an alligator.
Professor Twist could not but smile.
'You mean,' he said, 'a crocodile.'

Upon CLUNN

A rowle of Parchment *Clunn* about him beares,
Charg'd with the Armes of all his Ancestors:
And seems halfe ravisht, when he looks upon
That *Bar*, this *Bend*; that *Fess*, this *Cheveron*;
This *Manch*, that *Moone*; this *Martlet*, and that *Mound*;
This counterchange of *Perle* and *Diamond*.
What joy can *Clun* have in that Coat, or this,
When as his owne still out at elboes is?

THE TANK

'If I had a little money,' mused the Reverend
    Philip Fish,
'And could buy (without a scruple) any little thing
    I wish,
I would purchase an Aquarium, some moss and ferns
    and sand,
Some pretty shining pebbles, branching coral,
    seashells, and
At centre, a small cistern – made of glass – and placed,
    well, *so*:
      And filled with what in France is known as *eau*.

'It's really very singular; as soon as I'm asleep,
My dreams at once commit me to the wonders of
    the deep;
I wallow with the whale, or in profundities obscure
Disport with shapes no waking eye for terror could
    endure.
At times I am an octopus; at times I am a sprat;
    And there *is* a lot of ocean for a little fish like that!

'I had an uncle – Phineas Fish; but now that he's
    deceased
All hope of a small legacy has practically ceased.
But if a rich parishioner should tactfully suggest,

"Now, tell me, Father Fish, what little present you'd
        like *best*,"
Although I wouldn't *think* of it – could only smile my
        thanks,
    I'm *sure*, you know, my thoughts would turn to
        tanks!'

MISS CLEGG

Miss Clegg was accustomed to do as she wished,
    Upon Fate she was never a waiter;
And whenever she came upon water she fished,
    And always attired in a gaiter.

The word has a singular look, I agree,
    Yet is apt in the case of Miss Clegg;
Since from birth she a monopode happened to be,
    And you can't wear a pair on one leg.

Her foot was her basis then, while with her float
    She dangled a worm 'neath a willow;
Or, far out to sea, stood erect in a boat,
    And awaited a bite from the billow.

MAD DOGS AND ENGLISHMEN

In tropical climes there are certain times of day
When all the citizens retire
To tear their clothes off and perspire.
It's one of those rules that the greatest fools obey,
Because the sun is much too sultry
And one must avoid its ultry-violet ray.

Papalaka papalaka papalaka boo,
Papalaka papalaka papalaka boo,
Digariga digariga digariga doo,
Digariga digariga digariga doo.

The natives grieve when the white men leave their
        huts,
Because they're obviously definitely nuts!

Mad dogs and Englishmen
Go out in the midday sun.
The Japanese don't care to,
The Chinese wouldn't dare to,
Hindoos and Argentines sleep firmly from twelve
        to one,
But Englishmen detest a siesta.
In the Philippines
There are lovely screens

To protect you from the glare.
In the Malay States
There are hats like plates
Which the Britishers won't wear.
At twelve noon
The natives swoon
And no further work is done,
But mad dogs and Englishmen
Go out in the midday sun.

It's such a surprise for the Eastern eyes to see
That though the English are effete,
They're quite impervious to heat,
When the white man rides every native hides in glee,
Because the simple creatures hope he
Will impale his solar topee on a tree.

    Bolyboly bolyboly bolyboly baa,
    Bolyboly bolyboly bolyboly baa,
    Habaninny habaninny habaninny haa,
    Habaninny habaninny habaninny haa.

It seems such a shame
When the English claim
The earth
That they give rise to such hilarity and mirth.

Mad dogs and Englishmen
Go out in the midday sun.
The toughest Burmese bandit
Can never understand it.
In Rangoon the heat of noon
Is just what the natives shun.
They put their Scotch or Rye down
And lie down.
In a jungle town
Where the sun beats down
To the rage of man and beast
The English garb
Of the English sahib
Merely gets a bit more creased.
In Bangkok
At twelve o'clock
They foam at the mouth and run,
But mad dogs and Englishmen
Go out in the midday sun.

Mad dogs and Englishmen
Go out in the midday sun.
The smallest Malay rabbit
Deplores this stupid habit.
In Hongkong
They strike a gong
And fire off a noonday gun

To reprimand each inmate
Who's in late.
In the mangrove swamps
Where the python romps
There is peace from twelve till two.
Even caribous
Lie around and snooze,
For there's nothing else to do.
In Bengal
To move at all
Is seldom, if ever done,
But mad dogs and Englishmen
Go out in the midday sun.

NOËL COWARD

LINES FOR CUSCUSCARAWAY
AND MIRZA MURAD ALI BEG

How unpleasant to meet Mr Eliot!
With his features of clerical cut,
And his brow so grim
And his mouth so prim
And his conversation, so nicely
Restricted to What Precisely
And If and Perhaps and But.
How unpleasant to meet Mr Eliot!
With a bobtail cur
In a coat of fur
And a porpentine cat
And a wopsical hat:
How unpleasant to meet Mr Eliot!
     (Whether his mouth be open or shut).

POLITICS

YES AND NO

Oh would I were a politician,
Or else a person with a mission.
Heavens, how happy I could be
If only I were sure of me.

How would I strut, could I believe
That, out of all the sons of Eve,
God had granted this former youth
A binding option on His truth.

One side of the moon we've seen alone;
The other she has never shown.
What dreamless sleep, what sound digestion,
Were it the same with every question!

Sometimes with secret pride I sigh
To think how tolerant am I;
Then wonder which is really mine;
Tolerance, or a rubber spine?

THE LATEST DECALOGUE

Thou shalt have one God only; who
Would be at the expense of two?
No graven images may be
Worshipped, except the currency:
Swear not at all; for, for thy curse
Thine enemy is none the worse:
At church on Sunday to attend
Will serve to keep the world thy friend:
Honour thy parents; that is, all
From whom advancement may befall:
Thou shalt not kill; but need'st not strive
Officiously to keep alive:
Do not adultery commit;
Advantage rarely comes of it:
Thou shalt not steal; an empty feat,
When it's so lucrative to cheat:
Bear not false witness; let the lie
Have time on its own wings to fly:
Thou shalt not covet, but tradition
Approves all forms of competition.

I HAD A DUCK-BILLED PLATYPUS

I had a duck-billed platypus when I was up at Trinity,
With whom I soon discovered a remarkable affinity.
He used to live in lodgings with myself and
      Arthur Purvis,
And we all went up together for the Diplomatic Service.
I had a certain confidence, I own, in his ability,
He mastered all the subjects with remarkable facility;
And Purvis, though more dubious, agreed that he
      was clever,
But no one else imagined he had any chance whatever.
I failed to pass the interview, the Board with
      wry grimaces
Took exception to my boots and then objected to
      my braces,
And Purvis too was failed by an intolerant examiner
Who said he had his doubts as to his sock-suspenders'
      stamina.
The bitterness of failure was considerably mollified,
However, by the ease with which our platypus had
      qualified.
The wisdom of the choice, it soon appeared, was
      undeniable;
There never was a diplomat more thoroughly reliable.
He never made rash statements his enemies might hold
      him to,

He never stated anything, for no one ever told him to,
And soon he was appointed, so correct was his
    behaviour,
Our Minister (without Portfolio) to Trans-Moravia.
My friend was loved and honoured from the Andes to
    Esthonia,
He soon achieved a pact between Peru and Patagonia,
He never vexed the Russians nor offended the
    Rumanians,
He pacified the Letts and yet appeased the Lithuanians,
Won approval from his masters down in Downing Street
    so wholly, O,
He was soon to be rewarded with the grant of a
    Portfolio.

When, on the Anniversary of Greek Emancipation,
Alas! He laid an egg in the Bulgarian Legation.
This untoward occurrence caused unheard-of
    repercussions,
Giving rise to epidemics of sword-clanking in the
    Prussians.
The Poles began to threaten, and the Finns began to
    flap at him,
Directing all the blame for this unfortunate mishap at
    him;
While the Swedes withdrew entirely from the Anglo-
    Saxon dailies

The right of photographing the Aurora Borealis,
And, all efforts at rapprochement in the meantime
      proving barren,
The Japanese in self-defence annexed the Isle of Arran.
My platypus, once thought to be more cautious and
      more tentative
Than any other living diplomatic representative,
Was now a sort of warning to all diplomatic students
Of the risks attached to negligence, the perils of
      imprudence,
And, branded in the Honours List as 'Platypus,
      Dame Vera',
Retired, a lonely figure, to lay eggs at Bordighera.

PATRICK BARRINGTON

IN A COPY OF MORE'S (OR SHAW'S OR WELLS'S OR PLATO'S OR ANYBODY'S) *UTOPIA*

So this is Utopia, is it? Well
I beg your pardon, I thought it was Hell.

ON A GENERAL ELECTION

The accursèd power which stands on Privilege
(And goes with Women, and Champagne and Bridge)
Broke – and Democracy resumed her reign:
(Which goes with Bridge, and Women and
    Champagne).

HILAIRE BELLOC

THE SOLUTION

After the uprising of the 17th June
The Secretary of the Writers' Union
Had leaflets distributed in the Stalinallee
Stating that the people
Had forfeited the confidence of the government
And could win it back only
By redoubled efforts. Would it not be easier
In that case for the government
To dissolve the people
And elect another?

LOW DOWN SANDCASTLE BLUES

You can't have everything, I said as we drank tea.
No, you can't have everything. And I sipped my tea.
    You can't have anything, my friend answered me.

Yes, I've wrestled with an angel: there is no other kind.
I wrestled with an angel: that wrestling's the
        only kind.
    Any easier wrestling finally sends you blind.

Trouble's a stray dog that's mighty hard to lose:
if he latches on to you, he's mighty hard to lose
    but not even a dog joins in when you sing the blues.

A man told me I've no right to what I need.
He told me Oh yes, I've no right to what I need.
    He had all his rights and quivered under them like
        a reed.

If you've got the gift of seeing things from both sides
– it's an angel-wound, that curse of seeing things from
        both sides –
    then police beat you up in a sandcastle built between
        tides.

A MODEST POLITICIAN

Godolphin says he does not wish to swell
The Roll of Fame; and it is just as well.

EPITAPH ON A POLITICIAN

Here William lies, in truth; before he died
For forty mortal years in truth he lied!

LORD FINCHLEY

Lord Finchley tried to mend the Electric Light
Himself. It struck him dead: And serve him right!
It is the business of the wealthy man
To give employment to the artisan.

THE PACIFIST

Pale Ebenezer thought it wrong to fight,
But Roaring Bill (who killed him) thought it right.

THE WORLD STATE

Oh, how I love Humanity,
  With love so pure and pringlish,
And how I hate the horrid French,
  Who never will be English!

The International Idea,
  The largest and the clearest,
Is welding all the nations now,
  Except the one that's nearest.

This compromise has long been known,
  This scheme of partial pardons,
In ethical societies
  And small suburban gardens –

The villas and the chapels where
  I learned with little labour
The way to love my fellow-man
  And hate my next-door neighbour.

LORD LUNDY

*Who was too freely moved to tears, and thereby
ruined his political career*

Lord Lundy from his earliest years
Was far too freely moved to Tears.
For instance, if his Mother said,
'Lundy! It's time to go to Bed!'
He bellowed like a Little Turk.
Or if his father, Lord Dunquerque,
Said, 'Hi!' in a Commanding Tone,
'Hi, Lundy! Leave the Cat alone!'
Lord Lundy, letting go its tail,
Would raise so terrible a wail
As moved his Grandpapa the Duke
To utter the severe rebuke:
'When I, Sir! was a little Boy,
An Animal was not a Toy!'

His father's Elder Sister, who
Was married to a Parvenoo,
Confided to Her Husband, 'Drat!
The Miserable, Peevish Brat!
Why don't they drown the Little Beast?'
Suggestions which, to say the least,
Are not what we expect to hear
From Daughters of an English Peer.

His grandmamma, His Mother's Mother,
Who had some dignity or other,
The Garter, or no matter what,
I can't remember all the Lot!
Said, 'Oh! that I were Brisk and Spry
To give him that for which to cry!'
(An empty wish, alas! for she
Was Blind and nearly ninety-three).

The Dear old Butler thought – but there!
I really neither know nor care
For what the Dear Old Butler thought!
In my opinion, Butlers ought
To know their place, and not to play
The Old Retainer night and day.
I'm getting tired and so are you,
Let's cut the Poem into two!

(*Second Canto*)
It happened to Lord Lundy then,
As happens to so many men:
Towards the age of twenty-six,
They shoved him into politics;

In which profession he commanded
The income that his rank demanded
In turn as Secretary for
India, the Colonies, and War.
But very soon his friends began
To doubt if he were quite the man:
Thus, if a member rose to say
(As members do from day to day),
'Arising out of that reply . . .!'
Lord Lundy would begin to cry.
A Hint at harmless little jobs
Would shake him with convulsive sobs.

While as for Revelations, these
Would simply bring him to his knees,
And leave him whimpering like a child.
It drove his Colleagues raving wild!
They let him sink from Post to Post,
From fifteen hundred at the most
To eight, and barely six – and then
To be Curator of Big Ben! . . .
And finally there came a Threat
To oust him from the Cabinet!

The Duke – his aged grand-sire – bore
The shame till he could bear no more.
He rallied his declining powers,

Summoned the youth to Brackley Towers,
And bitterly addressed him thus –
'Sir! you have disappointed us!
We had intended you to be
The next Prime Minister but three:
The stocks were sold; the Press was squared;
The Middle Class was quite prepared.
But as it is! . . . My language fails!
Go out and govern New South Wales!'

The Aged Patriot groaned and died:
And gracious! how Lord Lundy cried!

THERE LIVED A KING

There lived a King, as I've been told,
In the wonder-working days of old,
When hearts were twice as good as gold,
   And twenty times as mellow.
Good-temper triumphed in his face,
And in his heart he found a place
For all the erring human race
   And every wretched fellow.
When he had Rhenish wine to drink
It made him very sad to think
That some, at junket or at jink,
   Must be content with toddy.
He wished all men as rich as he
(And he was rich as rich could be),
So to the top of every tree
   Promoted everybody.

Lord Chancellors were cheap as sprats,
And Bishops in their shovel hats
Were plentiful as tabby cats –
   In point of fact, too many.
Ambassadors cropped up like hay,
Prime Ministers and such as they
Grew like asparagus in May,
   And Dukes were three a penny.

On every side Field Marshals gleamed,
Small beer were Lords Lieutenant deemed,
With Admirals the ocean teemed
 All round his wide dominions.
And Party Leaders you might meet
In twos and threes in every street,
Maintaining, with no little heat,
 Their various opinions.

That King, although no one denies
His heart was of abnormal size,
Yet he'd have acted otherwise
 If he had been acuter.
The end is easily foretold,
When every blessed thing you hold
Is made of silver, or of gold,
 You long for simple pewter.
When you have nothing else to wear
But cloth of gold and satins rare,
For cloth of gold you cease to care –
 Up goes the price of shoddy.
In short, whoever you may be,
To this conclusion you'll agree,
When every one is somebodee,
 Then no one's anybody!

W. S. GILBERT   171

THE EWART ORGANIZATION

The Chairman's a charming graduate.
He does no work. He just inspires everybody.

The Deputy Chairman makes a few decisions.
He's very good at speaking after dinner.

The Managing Director shouts down the telephone.
His worries affect the lining of his stomach.

The executives wear dark suits, collars and ties.
They live their lives in memos of meetings.

The sales force whizz round the country in cars.
They sell soap even when the roads are icy.

The men on the factory floor are bored to extinction.
They're not alive, they go through the motions.

The secretaries are picked for their nubile attractions.
They type, varnish their nails, tell everything often.

There's a lot of life in the Ewart Organization.
Needless to say, I am the Chairman.

GUNS BEFORE BUTTER

1

The famous remark of General Goering
That guns should come before butter
Is correct inasmuch as the government needs
The more guns the less butter it has
For the less butter it has
The more enemies.

2

Furthermore it should be said that
Guns on an empty stomach
Are not to every people's taste.
Merely swallowing gas
They say, does not quench thirst
And without woollen pants
A soldier, it could be, is brave only in summer.

3

When the artillery runs out of ammunition
Officers up front tend
To get holes in their backs.

HIGH SUGAR

Honey gave sweetness
to Athens and Rome,
and later, when splendour
might rise nearer home,

sweetness was still honey
since, pious or lax,
every cloister had its apiary
for honey and wax

but when kings and new doctrines
drained those deep hives
then millions of people
were shipped from their lives

to grow the high sugar
from which were refined
frigates, perukes, human races
and the liberal mind.

LITERATURE

BLOOMSBURY SNAPSHOT

Virginia's writing her diary,
Vanessa is shelling the peas,
And Carrington's there, hiding under her hair,
And squinting, and painting the trees.

Well Maynard is smiling at Duncan,
A little to Lytton's distress,
But Ralph's lying down with a terrible frown
For he'd rather be back in the mess.

There's Ottoline, planning a party –
But Leonard's impassive as stone:
He knows that they'll all sit around in deck chairs,
Discussing their own and each other's affaires,
And forming, perhaps, into new sets of pairs:
And oh, how the bookshelves will groan.

REPROOF DESERVED, *OR* AFTER
THE LECTURE

When I saw the grapefruit drying, cherry in each
    centre lying,
  And a dozen guests expected at the table's polished
    oak,
Then I knew, my lecture finished, I'ld be feeling quite
    diminished
  Talking on, but unprotected, so that all my spirit
    broke.

'Have you read the last Charles Morgan?' 'Are you
    writing for the organ
  Which is published as a vital adjunct to our cultural
    groups?'
'This year some of us are learning all *The Lady's Not
    for Burning*
  For a poetry recital we are giving to the troops.'

'Mr Betjeman, I grovel before critics of the novel,
  Tell me, if I don't offend you, have you written one
    yourself?
You haven't? Then the one I wrote is (not that I expect
    a notice)
  Something I would like to send you, just for keeping
    on your shelf.'

'Betjeman, I bet your racket brings you in a pretty
        packet
    Raising the old lecture curtain, writing titbits here
        and there.
But, by Jove, your hair is thinner, since you came to us
        in Pinner,
    And you're fatter now, I'm certain. What you need is
        country air.'

This and that way conversation, till in desperation
    To a kind face (can I doubt it?) mercifully mute
        so far.
'Oh,' it says, 'I missed the lecture, wasn't it on
        architecture?
    Do please tell me all about it, what you do and who
        you are.'

THE BLACK BOX

As well as these poor poems
I am writing some wonderful ones.
They are all being filed separately,
nobody sees them.

When I die they will be buried
in a big black tin box.
In fifty years' time
they must be dug up,

for so my will provides.
This is to confound the critics
and teach everybody
a valuable lesson.

CACOËTHES SCRIBENDI

If all the trees in all the woods were men,
And each and every blade of grass a pen;
If every leaf on every shrub and tree
Turned to a sheet of foolscap; every sea
Were changed to ink, and all earth's living tribes
Had nothing else to do but act as scribes,
And for ten thousand ages, day and night,
The human race should write, and write, and write,
Till all the pens and paper were used up,
And the huge inkstand was an empty cup,
Still would the scribblers clustered round its brink
Call for more pens, more paper, and more ink.

OLIVER WENDELL HOLMES

ON HIS BOOKS

When I am dead, I hope it may be said:
'His sins were scarlet, but his books were read.'

HILAIRE BELLOC

From THE SECOND PART OF ABSALOM
AND ACHITOPHEL

Now stop your noses Readers, all and some,
For here's a tun of Midnight-work to come,
Og from a Treason Tavern rowling home.
Round as a Globe, and Liquor'd ev'ry chink,
Goodly and Great he Sayls behind his Link;
With all this Bulk there's nothing lost in *Og*
For ev'ry inch that is not Fool is Rogue:
A Monstrous mass of foul corrupted matter,
As all the Devils had spew'd to make the batter.
When wine has given him courage to Blaspheme,
He Curses God, but God before Curst him;
And if man cou'd have reason none has more,
That made his Paunch so rich and him so poor.
With wealth he was not trusted, for Heav'n knew
What 'twas of Old to pamper up a *Jew*;
To what wou'd he on Quail and Pheasant swell,
That ev'n on Tripe and Carrion cou'd rebell?
But though Heav'n made him poor (with rev'rence
        speaking)
He never was a Poet of God's making;
The Midwife laid her hand on his Thick Skull,
With this Prophetick blessing – *Be thou Dull*;
Drink, Swear and Roar, forbear no lewd delight
Fit for thy Bulk, doe any thing but write:

Thou art of lasting Make like thoughtless men,
A strong Nativity – but for the Pen;
Eat Opium, mingle Arsenick in thy Drink,
Still thou mayst live avoiding Pen and Ink.
I see, I see 'tis Counsell given in vain,
For Treason botcht in Rhime will be thy bane;
Rhime is the Rock on which thou art to wreck,
'Tis fatal to thy Fame and to thy Neck:
Why should thy Metre good King *David* blast?
A Psalm of his will Surely be thy last.
Dar'st thou presume in verse to meet thy foes,
Thou whom the Penny Pamphlet foil'd in prose?
Doeg, whom God for Mankind's mirth has made,
O'er-tops thy tallent in thy very Trade;
Doeg to thee, thy paintings are so Course,
A Poet is, though he's the Poet's Horse.
A Double Noose thou on thy Neck dost pull,
For Writing Treason, and for Writing dull;
To die for Faction is a Common evil,
But to be hang'd for Non-sense is the Devil:
Hadst thou the Glories of thy King exprest,
Thy praises had been Satyr at the best;
But thou in Clumsy verse, unlickt, unpointed,
Hast Shamefully defi'd the Lord's Anointed:

I will not rake the Dunghill of thy Crimes,
For who wou'd read thy Life that reads thy rhimes?
But of King *David*'s Foes be this the Doom,
May all be like the Young-man *Absalom*;
And for my Foes may this their Blessing be,
To talk like *Doeg*, and to Write like Thee.

JOHN DRYDEN

You cannot hope
   to bribe or twist,
thank God! the
   British journalist.

But, seeing what
   the man will do
unbribed, there's
   no occasion to.

HUMBERT WOLFE

A critic is a creature who has views
Quite like a camel's: flowers and fruit he scorns.
In the flower-garden of the honeyed Muse
He starves unless he finds a meal of thorns.

184   BHARTṚHARI
     TRANS. JOHN BROUGH

ON A LADY WHO P—ST AT THE TRAGEDY OF CATO
Occasion'd by an epigram on a lady who wept at it

While maudlin Whigs deplor'd their *Cato*'s Fate,
Still with dry Eyes the Tory *Celia* sate,
But while her Pride forbids her Tears to flow,
The gushing Waters find a Vent below:
Tho' secret, yet with copious Grief she mourns,
Like twenty River-Gods with all their Urns.
Let others screw their Hypocritick Face,
She shews her Grief in a sincerer Place;
There Nature reigns, and Passion void of Art,
For that Road leads directly to the Heart.

ALEXANDER POPE

ACADEMIC

The stethoscope tells what everyone fears:
You're likely to go on living for years,
With a nurse-maid waddle and a shop-girl simper,
And the style of your prose growing limper and limper.

THEODORE ROETHKE

TO MINERVA

My temples throb, my pulses boil,
    I'm sick of Song, and Ode, and Ballad –
So, Thyrsis, take the Midnight Oil,
    And pour it on a lobster salad.

My brain is dull, my sight is foul,
    I cannot write a verse, or read –
Then, Pallas, take away thine Owl,
    And let us have a lark instead.

THOMAS HOOD

PHILOLOGICAL

The British puss demurely mews;
His transatlantic kin meow.
The kine in Minnesota moo;
Not so the gentle Devon cows:
       They low,
As every schoolchild ought to know.

THE UNCERTAINTY
OF THE POET

*'The Tate Gallery yesterday announced that it had
paid £1 million for a Giorgio de Chirico masterpiece,*
The Uncertainty of the Poet. *It depicts a torso and
a bunch of bananas.' (Guardian, 2 April 1985)*

I am a poet.
I am very fond of bananas.

I am bananas.
I am very fond of a poet.

I am a poet of bananas.
I am very fond,

A fond poet of 'I am, I am' –
Very bananas,

Fond of 'Am I bananas,
Am I?' – a very poet.

Bananas of a poet!
Am I fond? Am I very?

Poet bananas! I am.
I am fond of a 'very'.

I am of very fond bananas.
Am I a poet?

WENDY COPE   187

BESTIARY

THE PIG

It was an evening in November,
As I very well remember,
I was strolling down the street in drunken pride,
But my knees were all a-flutter,
And I landed in the gutter
And a pig came up and lay down by my side.

Yes, I lay there in the gutter
Thinking thoughts I could not utter,
When a colleen passing by did softly say
'You can tell a man who boozes
By the company he chooses' –
And the pig got up and slowly walked away.

ANON.

THE WASP

The wasp and all his numerous family
I look upon as a major calamily,
He throws open his nest with prodigality,
But I distrust his waspitality.

OGDEN NASH   191

THE FROG PRINCE

I am a frog
I live under a spell
I live at the bottom
Of a green well

And here I must wait
Until a maiden places me
On her royal pillow
And kisses me
In her father's palace.

The story is familiar
Everybody knows it well
But do other enchanted people feel as nervous
As I do? The stories do not tell,

Ask if they will be happier
When the changes come
As already they are fairly happy
In a frog's doom?

I have been a frog now
For a hundred years
And in all this time
I have not shed many tears,

I am happy, I like the life,
Can swim for many a mile
(When I have hopped to the river)
And am for ever agile.

And the quietness,
Yes, I like to be quiet
I am habituated
To a quiet life,

But always when I think these thoughts
As I sit in my well
Another thought comes to me and says:
It is part of the spell

To be happy
To work up contentment
To make much of being a frog
To fear disenchantment

Says, It will be *heavenly*
To be set free,
Cries, *Heavenly* the girl who disenchants
And the royal times, *heavenly,*
And I think it will be.

Come then, royal girl and royal times,
Come quickly,
I can be happy until you come
But I cannot be heavenly,
Only disenchanted people
Can be heavenly.

STEVIE SMITH

THE FROG

Be kind and tender to the Frog,
    And do not call him names,
As 'Slimy skin', or 'Polly-wog',
    Or likewise 'Ugly James',
Or 'Gape-a-grin', or 'Toad-gone-wrong',
    Or 'Billy Bandy-knees':

The Frog is justly sensitive
    To epithets like these.
No animal will more repay
    A treatment kind and fair;
At least so lonely people say
Who keep a frog (and, by the way,
They are extremely rare).

THE OCTOPUS

Tell me, O Octopus, I begs,
Is those things arms, or is they legs?
I marvel at thee, Octopus;
If I were thou, I'd call me Us.

THE EEL

I don't mind eels
Except as meals.
And the way they feels.

OGDEN NASH

THE RABBIT

The rabbit has a charming face:
Its private life is a disgrace.
I really dare not name to you
The awful things that rabbits do;
Things that your paper never prints –
You only mention them in hints.
They have such lost, degraded souls
No wonder they inhabit holes;
When such depravity is found
It only can live underground.

ANON.

TO A MOUSE

Wee, sleekit, cowrin', tim'rous beastie,
Oh, what a panic's in thy breastie!
Thou needna start awa' sae hasty,
         Wi' bick'ring brattle!
I wad be laith to rin and chase thee,
         Wi' murd'ring pattle!

I'm truly sorry man's dominion
Has broken nature's social union,
And justifies that ill opinion
         Which mak's thee startle
At me, thy poor earth-born companion,
         And fellow-mortal!

I doubt na, whyles, but thou may thieve;
What then? poor beastie, thou maun live
A daimen icker in a thrave
         'S a sma' request:
I'll get a blessin' wi' the lave,
         And never miss't!

Thy wee bit housie, too, in ruin!
It's silly wa's the win's are strewin'!
And naething now to big a new ane
         O' foggage green!

And bleak December's winds ensuin',
                    Baith snell and keen!

Thou saw the fields laid bare and waste,
And weary winter comin' fast,
And cozie here, beneath the blast
                    Thou thought to dwell,
Till, crash! the cruel coulter past
                    Out through thy cell.

That wee bit heap o' leaves and stibble
Has cost thee mony a weary nibble!
Now thou's turned out for a' thy trouble,
                    But house or hauld,
To thole the winter's sleety dribble,
                    And cranreuch cauld!

But, Mousie, thou art no thy lane
In proving foresight may be vain!
The best-laid schemes o' mice and men
                    Gang aft a-gley,
And lea'e us nought but grief and pain
                    For promised joy.

Still thou art blest, compared wi' me!
The present only toucheth thee:
But, och! I backward cast my e'e
                    On prospects drear!
And forward, though I canna see,
                    I guess and fear.

ROBERT BURNS

MOUSE

Beautiful days, time's mice, gnawing
Little by little my life away.
God! Nearly twenty-eight this spring,
And misspent years too, I should say.

CARP

In your fish-pools and your ponds
O carp, how your lives are long!
Does death forget that you're his dish,
O most melancholy fish?

198   GUILLAUME APOLLINAIRE
      TRANS. ANNE HYDE GREET

EPIGRAM III.35

Instant Fish
by Phidias!
Add water
and they swim.

MARTIAL, TRANS. PETER PORTER

TO A FISH

You strange, astonished-looking, angle-faced,
   Dreary-mouthed, gaping wretches of the sea,
   Gulping salt-water everlastingly,
Cold-blooded, though with red your blood be graced,
And mute, though dwellers in the roaring waste;
   And you, all shapes beside, that fishy be, –
   Some round, some flat, some long, all devilry,
Legless, unloving, infamously chaste; –

O scaly, slippery, wet, swift, staring wights,
   What is't ye do? What life lead? eh, dull goggles?
How do ye vary your vile days and nights?
   How pass your Sundays? Are ye still but joggles
Is ceaseless wash? Still nought but gapes, and bites,
   And drinks, and stares, diversified with boggles?

LEIGH HUNT

A FISH ANSWERS

Amazing monster! that, for aught I know,
    With the first sight of thee didst make our race
    For ever stare! O flat and shocking face,
Grimly divided from the breast below!
Thou that on dry land horribly dost go
    With a split body and most ridiculous pace,
    Prong after prong, disgracer of all grace,
Long-useless-finned, haired, upright, unwet, slow!

O breather of unbreathable, sword-sharp air,
    How canst exist? How bear thyself, thou dry
And dreary sloth? What particle canst share
    Of the only blessed life, the watery?
I sometimes see of ye an actual *pair*
    Go by! linked fin by fin! most odiously.

THE PYTHON

A Python I should not advise –
It needs a doctor for its eyes
And has the measles yearly.
However, if you feel inclined
To get one (to improve your mind,
And not from fashion merely),
Allow no music near its cage;
And when it flies into a rage
Chastise it, most severely.

I had an aunt in Yucatan
Who bought a Python from a man
   And kept it for a pet.
She died, because she never knew
Those simple little rules and few –
   The Snake is living yet.

THE COBRA

This creature fills its mouth with venum
And walks upon its duodenum.
He who attempts to tease the cobra
Is soon a sadder he, and sobra.

OGDEN NASH

AN APPEAL TO CATS IN THE BUSINESS OF LOVE

Ye cats that at midnight spit at each other,
Who best feel the pangs of a passionate lover,
I appeal to your scratches and your tattered fur
If the business of love be no more than to purr?
Old Lady Grimalkin with her gooseberry eyes
Knew something when a kitten – for why? she was wise;
You find by experience the love-fit's soon o'er:
Puss-puss! lasts not long but turns to Cat-whore!
        Men ride many miles,
        Cats tread many tiles,
    Both hazard their necks in the fray;
        Only cats, when they fall
        From a house or a wall,
    Keep their feet, mount their tails, and away!

202 THOMAS FLATMAN

THE BLIND SHEEP

The Sheep is blind; a passing Owl,
A surgeon of some local skill,
Has undertaken, for a fee,
The cure. A stump, his surgery,
Is licked clean by a Cat; his tools –
A tooth, a thorn, some battered nails –
He ranges by a shred of sponge
And he is ready to begin.
Pushed forward through the gaping crowd,
'Wait,' bleats the Sheep; 'all is prepared?'
The Owl lists forceps, scalpel, lancet –
The old Sheep interrupts his answer;
'These lesser things may all be well;
But tell me, friend – how goes the world?'
The Owl says blankly: 'You will find it
Goes as it went ere you were blinded.'
'What?' cries the Sheep. 'Then take your fee
But cure some other fool, not me:
To witness that enormity
I would not give a blade of grass.
I am a Sheep, and not an Ass.'

THE GRACKLE

The grackle's voice is less than mellow,
His heart is black, his eye is yellow,
He bullies more attractive birds
With hoodlum deeds and vulgar words,
And should a human interfere,
Attacks that human in the rear.
I cannot help but deem the grackle
An ornithological debacle.

THE HIPPOPOTAMUS

Behold the hippopotamus!
We laugh at how he looks to us,
And yet in moments dank and grim
I wonder how we look to him.
Peace, peace, thou hippopotamus!
We really look all right to us,
As you no doubt delight the eye
Of other hippopotami.

THE HIPPOPOTAMUS SONG

A bold Hippopotamus was standing one day
On the banks of the cool Shalimar.
He gazed at the bottom as it peacefully lay
By the light of the evening star.
Away on a hilltop sat combing her hair
His fair Hippopotamine maid;
The Hippopotamus was no ignoramus
And sang her this sweet serenade.

    Mud, Mud, glorious mud,
    Nothing quite like it for cooling the blood!
    So follow me, follow
    Down to the hollow
    And there let us wallow
    In glorious mud!

The fair Hippopotama he aimed to entice
From her seat on the hilltop above,
As she hadn't got a ma to give her advice,
Came tiptoeing down to her love.
Like thunder the forest re-echoed the sound
Of the song that they sang as they met.
His inamorata adjusted her garter
And lifted her voice in duet.

Mud, Mud, glorious mud,
Nothing quite like it for cooling the blood!
So follow me, follow,
Down to the hollow
And there let us wallow
In glorious mud!

Now more Hippopotami began to convene
On the banks of that river so wide.
I wonder now what am I to say of the scene
That ensued by the Shalimar side?
They dived all at once with an ear-splitting splosh
Then rose to the surface again,
A regular army of Hippopotami
All singing this haunting refrain.

Mud! Mud! Glorious mud!
Nothing quite like it for cooling the blood.
So follow me, follow,
Down to the hollow
And there let us wallow
In glorious mud!

MOLLUSC

By its nobship sailing upside down,
by its inner sexes, by the crystalline
pimplings of its skirts, by the sucked-on
lifelong kiss of its toppling motion,
by the viscose optics now extruded
now wizened instantaneously, by the
ridges grating up a food-path, by
the pop shell in its nick of dry,
by excretion, the earthworm coils, the glibbing,
by the gilt slipway, and by pointing
perhaps as far back into time as
ahead, a shore being folded interior,
by boiling on salt, by coming uncut over
a razor's edge, by hiding the Oligocene
underleaf may this and every snail sense
itself ornament the weave of presence.

EPIGRAM

engraved on the collar of a dog which I gave to his Royal Highness Frederick Prince of Wales

I am his Highness' dog at Kew.
Pray tell me, sir, whose dog are you?

ALEXANDER POPE

THE DOG

The truth I do not stretch or shove
When I state the dog is full of love.
I've also proved, by actual test,
A wet dog is the lovingest.

THE COW

The cow is of the bovine ilk;
One end is moo, the other, milk.

THE LOUSE

On seeing one on a lady's bonnet at church

Ha! whare ye gaun, ye crowlin' ferlie!
Your impudence protects you sairly:
I canna say but ye strunt rarely
          Owre gauze and lace;
Though faith, I fear ye dine but sparely
          On sic a place.

Ye ugly, creepin', blastit wonner,
Detested, shunned by saunt an' sinner,
How dare ye set your fit upon her,
          Sae fine a lady!
Gae somewhere else and seek your dinner
          On some poor body.

Swith, in some beggar's haffet squattle;
There ye may creep, and sprawl, and sprattle
Wi' ither kindred jumpin' cattle,
          In shoals and nations;
Whare horn or bane ne'er dare unsettle
          Your thick plantations.

ROBERT BURNS   209

THE BUNYIP

Feathered and gray, about the size
Of a full-grown calf, its long neck
Budded with an emu's head, covered

With fur. The voice (reportedly) is like
A thousand booming drums. It puzzled aborigines
Long before the white man came.

It lives in the sea. Its names
Are musical: Tumbata, Bunyip,
Kanjaprati, Melagi. From its back

A plume of water spouts, the terror of
The womenfolk of fishermen.
It crosses oceans into inland waters,

Crying sometimes, after dark, that it is not
Extinct, imaginary, or a myth –
Its feathers ruffled, and its voice

Not like a thousand drums at all,
But muffled, dwindling, hard to hear these nights
Like far-off foghorns that the wind throws back.

MORTALITY

OPPORTUNITY

When Mrs Gorm (Aunt Eloïse)
Was stung to death by savage bees,
Her husband (Prebendary Gorm)
Put on his veil, and took the swarm.
He's publishing a book next May
On 'How to Make Bee-keeping Pay'.

MR JONES

'There's been an accident,' they said,
'Your servant's cut in half; he's dead!'
'Indeed!' said Mr Jones, 'and please,
Send me the half that's got my keys.'

L'ENFANT GLACÉ

When Baby's cries grew hard to bear,
I popped him in the Frigidaire.
I never would have done so if
I'd known that he'd be frozen stiff.
My wife said: 'George, I'm so unhappé
Our darling's now completely *frappé*!'

NOTHING TO FEAR

All fixed: early arrival at the flat
Lent by a friend, whose note says *Lucky sod*;
Drinks on the tray; the cover-story pat
And quite uncheckable; her husband off
Somewhere with all the kids till six o'clock
(Which ought to be quite long enough);
And all worth while: face really beautiful,
Good legs and hips, and as for breasts – my God.
What about guilt, compunction and such stuff?
I've had my fill of all that cock;
It'll wear off, as usual.

Yes, all fixed. Then why this slight trembling,
Dry mouth, quick pulse-rate, sweaty hands,
As though she were the first? No, not impatience,
Nor fear of failure, thank you, Jack.
Beauty, they tell me, is a dangerous thing,
Whose touch will burn, but I'm asbestos, see?
All worth while – it's a dead coincidence
That sitting here, a bag of glands
Tuned up to concert pitch, I seem to sense
A different style of caller at my back,
As cold as ice, but just as set on me.

MY DAD WAS WORRIED

My Dad was worried about his brother,
  frightened he wouldn't live long,
  so he went to every astrologer in town
and got the same report – nothing to worry about
  he'll live to a ripe old age.
Only Hermoclides foretold his early death
  but that was at the funeral.

LEAN GAIUS

Lean Gaius, who was thinner than a straw
And who could slip through even a locked door,
Is dead, and we his friends are twice bereft,
In losing him and finding nothing left
To put into the coffin: what they'll do
In Hades with a creature who is too
Shadowy to be a Shade, God knows,
But when we bear him to his last repose,
We'll make it stylish – mourners, black crêpe, bier,
The lot, and though he won't himself appear,
His empty coffin's progress will be pious –
THE DEATH OF NOTHING, FUNERAL OF GAIUS!

LUCILIUS   215
TRANS. PETER PORTER

TO HIS SKELETON

Why will you vex me with
These bone-spurs in the ear,
With X-rayed phlebolith
And calculus? See here,

Noblest of armatures,
The grin which bares my teeth
Is mine as yet, not yours.
Did you not stand beneath

This flesh, I could not stand,
But would revert to slime
Informous and unmanned;
And I may come in time

To wish your peace my fate,
Your sculpture my renown.
Still, I have held you straight
And mean to lay you down

Without too much disgrace
When what can perish dies.
For now then, keep your place
And do not colonize.

ARITHMETIC ON THE FRONTIER

A great and glorious thing it is
    To learn, for seven years or so,
The Lord knows what of that and this,
    Ere reckoned fit to face the foe –
The flying bullet down the Pass,
That whistles clear: 'All flesh is grass.'

Three hundred pounds per annum spent
    On making brain and body meeter
For all the murderous intent
    Comprised in 'villainous saltpetre'!
And after? – Ask the Yusufzaies
What comes of all our 'ologies.

A scrimmage in a Border Station –
    A canter down some dark defile –
Two thousand pounds of education
    Drops to a ten-rupee jezail –
The Crammer's boast, the Squadron's pride,
Shot like a rabbit in a ride!

No proposition Euclid wrote
    No formulae the text-books know,
Will turn the bullet from your coat,
    Or ward the tulwar's downward blow.

Strike hard who cares – shoot straight who can –
The odds are on the cheaper man.

One sword-knot stolen from the camp
   Will pay for all the school expenses
Of any Kurrum Valley scamp
   Who knows no word of moods and tenses,
But, being blessed with perfect sight,
Picks off our messmates left and right.

With home-bred hordes the hillsides teem.
   The troopships bring us one by one,
At vast expense of time and steam,
   To slay Afridis where they run.
The 'captives of our bow and spear'
Are cheap, alas! as we are dear.

WASTE

I had written to Aunt Maud,
Who was on a trip abroad,
When I heard she'd died of cramp
Just too late to save the stamp.

HARRY GRAHAM

YES, I KNOW

That pale face stretches across the centuries
It is so subtle and yielding; yet innocent,
Her name is Lucretia Borgia.

Yes, I know. I knew her brother Cesare
Once. But only for a short time.

ALL THINGS PASS

All things pass
Love and mankind is grass.

STEVIE SMITH

A TOCCATA OF GALUPPI'S

Oh Galuppi, Baldassaro, this is very sad to find!
I can hardly misconceive you; it would prove me deaf
    and blind;
But although I take your meaning, 'tis with such a
    heavy mind!

Here you come with your old music, and here's all the
    good it brings.
What, they lived once thus at Venice where the
    merchants were the kings,
Where Saint Mark's is, where the Doges used to wed
    the sea with rings?

Ay, because the sea's the street there; and 'tis arched by
    . . . what you call
. . . Shylock's bridge with houses on it, where they kept
    the carnival:
I was never out of England – it's as if I saw it all.

Did young people take their pleasure when the sea was
    warm in May?
Balls and masks begun at midnight, burning ever to
    mid-day,
When they made up fresh adventures for the morrow,
    do you say?

Was a lady such a lady, cheeks so round and lips
    so red, –
On her neck the small face buoyant, like a bell-flower
    on its bed,
O'er the breast's superb abundance where a man might
    base his head?

Well, and it was graceful of them – they'd break talk off
    and afford
– She, to bite her mask's black velvet – he, to finger on
    his sword,
While you sat and played Toccatas, stately at the
    clavichord?

What? Those lesser thirds so plaintive, sixths
    diminished, sigh on sigh,
Told them something? Those suspensions, those
    solutions – 'Must we die?'
Those commiserating sevenths – 'Life might last! we
    can but try!'

'Were you happy?' – 'Yes.' – 'And are you still as
    happy?' – 'Yes. And you?'
– 'Then, more kisses!' – 'Did *I* stop them, when a
    million seemed so few?'
Hark, the dominant's persistence till it must be
    answered to!

So, an octave struck the answer. Oh, they praised you,
    I dare say!
'Brave Galuppi! that was music! good alike at grave
    and gay!
'I can always leave off talking when I hear a master
    play!'

Then they left you for their pleasure: till in due time,
    one by one,
Some with lives that came to nothing, some with deeds
    as well undone,
Death stepped tacitly and took them where they never
    see the sun.

But when I sit down to reason, think to take my stand
    nor swerve,
While I triumph o'er a secret wrung from nature's
    close reserve,
In you come with your cold music till I creep thro'
    every nerve.

Yes, you, like a ghostly cricket, creaking where a house
    was burned:
'Dust and ashes, dead and done with, Venice spent
    what Venice earned.
'The soul, doubtless, is immortal – where a soul can be
    discerned.

'Yours for instance: you know physics, something
    of geology,
'Mathematics are your pastime; souls shall rise in their
    degree;
'Butterflies may dread extinction, – you'll not die,
    it cannot be!

'As for Venice and her people, merely born to bloom
    and drop,
Here on earth they bore their fruitage, mirth and folly
    were the crop:
'What of soul was left, I wonder, when the kissing had
    to stop?

'Dust and ashes!' So you creak it, and I want the heart
    to scold.
Dear dead women, with such hair, too – what's become
    of all the gold
Used to hang and brush their bosoms? I feel chilly and
    grown old.

Give me a doctor, partridge-plump,
Short in the leg and broad in the rump,
An endomorph with gentle hands,
Who'll never make absurd demands
That I abandon all my vices,
Nor pull a long face in a crisis,
But with a twinkle in his eye
Will tell me that I have to die.

ON MARY ANN

Mary Ann has gone to rest,
Safe at last on Abraham's breast,
Which may be nuts for Mary Ann,
But is certainly rough on Abraham.

ON WILL SMITH

Here lies Will Smith – and, what's something
    rarish,
He was born, bred, and hanged, all in the same
    parish

AT POTTERNE, WILTSHIRE

Here lies Mary, the wife of John Ford,
We hope her soul is gone to the Lord;
But if for Hell she has chang'd this life
She had better be there than be John Ford's wife.

ANON. 225

EPIGRAM I.16

Aper the expert archer accidentally shot
His rich wife in the heart.

He was lucky. She was not.

MARTIAL
TRANS. RICHARD O'CONNELL

EPITAPH ON CHARLES II

Here lies our Sovereign Lord the King,
    Whose word no man relies on,
Who never said a foolish thing,
    Nor ever did a wise one.

JOHN WILMOT, EARL OF ROCHESTER

HERE LIES A PHILOSOPHER

Here lies a philosopher, knowing and brave,
    From whom Madam Nature ne'er hid the least wonder,
Who looking to heaven, tumbled into his grave,
    And disdain'd that same earth which he rotting
    lies under.

226   CHARLES DIBDIN

The angler rose, he took his rod,
He kneeled and made his prayers to God.
The living God sat overhead:
The angler tripped, the eels were fed.

R. L. STEVENSON

EPITAPH ON AN UNFORTUNATE ARTIST

He found a formula for drawing comic rabbits:
  The formula for drawing comic rabbits paid,
So in the end he could not change the tragic habits
  This formula for drawing comic rabbits made.

ROBERT GRAVES

From TOMBSTONES IN THE STARLIGHT

THE PRETTY LADY

She hated bleak and wintry things alone.
    All that was warm and quick, she loved too well –
A light, a flame, a heart against her own;
    It is forever bitter cold, in Hell.

THE VERY RICH MAN

He'd have the best, and that was none too good;
    No barrier could hold, before his terms.
He lies below, correct in cypress wood,
    And entertains the most exclusive worms.

THE FISHERWOMAN

The man she had was kind and clean
    And well enough for every day,
But, oh, dear friends, you should have seen
    The one that got away!

THE ACTRESS

Her name, cut clear upon this marble cross,
    Shines, as it shone when she was still on earth;
While tenderly the mild, agreeable moss
    Obscures the figures of her date of birth.

A DENTIST

Stranger! Approach this spot with gravity!
John Brown is filling his last cavity.

AT GREAT TORRINGTON, DEVON

Here lies a man who was killed by lightning;
He died when his prospects seemed to be brightening.
He might have cut a flash in this world of trouble,
But the flash cut him, and he lies in the stubble.

AT ABERDEEN

Here lie I, Martin Elginbrodde:
Have mercy o' my soul, Lord God,
As I wad do, were I Lord God,
And ye were Martin Elginbrodde.

ANON.   229

EPITAPH IN ST OLAVE'S' SOUTHWARK, ON MR MUNDAY

Hallowed be the Sabbaoth,
And farewell all wordly Pelfe;
The Weeke begins on Tuesday,
For Munday hath hang'd himselfe.

ON A TIRED HOUSEWIFE

Here lies a poor woman who was always tired,
She lived in a house where help wasn't hired:
Her last words on earth were: 'Dear friends, I am going
To where there's no cooking, or washing, or sewing,
For everything there is exact to my wishes,
For where they don't eat there's no washing of dishes.
I'll be where loud anthems will always be ringing,
But having no voice I'll be quit of the singing.
Don't mourn for me now, don't mourn for me never,
I am going to do nothing for ever and ever.'

ACKNOWLEDGMENTS

Thanks are due to the following copyright holders for their permission to reprint:

AMIS, KINGSLEY: 'Nothing to Fear' from *Collected Poems 1944–1979* by Kingsley Amis. Copyright © 1967 Kingsley Amis. Reprinted by kind permission of Jonathan Clowes Ltd, London, on behalf of the Literary Estate of Sir Kingsley Amis. APOLLINAIRE, GUILLAUME: 'Hotel', 'Carp', 'Mouse' and 'In this mirror' from *Alcools*, translated by Anne Hyde Greet. Copyright © 1965 The Regents of the University of California and the University of California Press. AUDEN, W. H.: 'Give me a doctor, partridge plump', 'A Young Person came out of the mists' and 'As the poets have mournfully sung' from *Shorts* in *Collected Shorter Poems 1927–1957* by W. H. Auden. From *Academic Graffiti*: 'Henry Adams', 'Lord Byron', 'Henry James', 'Karl Marx' and 'Cardinal Newman'; 'Smelt and Tasted', 'Heard and Seen' from *Collected Poems* by W. H. Auden. Reprinted by kind permission of Faber and Faber Ltd in the UK. And in the US: 'Heard and Seen', copyright © 1969 by W. H. Auden; 'Smelt and Tasted', copyright © 1969 by W. H. Auden; 'Shorts', copyright © 1974 by The Estate of W. H. Auden; 'Academic Grafitti', copyright © 1960 by W. H. Auden, from *W. H. Auden: Collected Poems* by W. H. Auden. Used by permission of Random House, Inc. BELLOC, HILAIRE: 'Tarantella', 'The Python', 'Juliet', 'Fatigue', 'The Frog', 'On His Books', 'The Pacifist', 'Lord Lundy', 'On a General Election', 'Lord Finchley', 'A Modest Politician', 'Epitaph on a Politician' and 'Henry King' from *Complete Verse* by Hilaire Belloc, © The Estate of Hilaire Belloc, 1970. Reprinted by permission of P.F.D. on behalf of The Estate of

INDEX OF AUTHORS